Certified

B

Corporation

Declaration of Interdependence

We envision a new sector of the economy

which harnesses the power of private enterprise to create public benefit.

This sector is comprised of a new type of corporation — the B Corporation —

which is purpose-driven, and creates benefit for all stakeholders, not just shareholders.

As members of this emerging sector and as entrepreneurs and investors in B Corporations,

We hold these truths to be self-evident:

That we must be the change we seek in the world.

That all business ought to be conducted as if people and place mattered.

That, through their products, practices, and profits, businesses should aspire

to do no harm and benefit all.

To do so requires that we act with the understanding that we are each dependent

upon another and thus responsible for each other and future generations.

B the change

The
B Corp
Handbook

How to
Use Business as
a Force for Good

Ryan Honeyman

Foreword by the Cofounders of B Lab

Berrett–Koehler Publishers, Inc.
San Francisco
a BK Business book

Berrett-Koehler Publishers, Inc.
235 Montgomery Street, Suite 650
San Francisco, CA 94104-2916
Tel: (415) 288-0260   Fax: (415) 362-2512   www.bkconnection.com

ORDERING INFORMATION

Quantity sales. Special discounts are available on quantity purchases by corporations, associations, and others. For details, contact the "Special Sales Department" at the Berrett-Koehler address above.

Individual sales. Berrett-Koehler publications are available through most bookstores. They can also be ordered directly from Berrett-Koehler: Tel: (800) 929-2929; Fax: (802) 864-7626; www.bkconnection.com

Orders for college textbook/course adoption use. Please contact Berrett-Koehler: Tel: (800) 929-2929; Fax: (802) 864-7626.

Orders by U.S. trade bookstores and wholesalers. Please contact Ingram Publisher Services, Tel: (800) 509-4887; Fax: (800) 838-1149; E-mail: customer.service @ingrampublisherservices.com; or visit www.ingrampublisherservices.com/Ordering for details about electronic ordering.

Berrett-Koehler and the BK logo are registered trademarks of Berrett-Koehler Publishers, Inc.

Printed in the United States of America

Berrett-Koehler books are printed on long-lasting acid-free paper. When it is available, we choose paper that has been manufactured by environmentally responsible processes. These may include using trees grown in sustainable forests, incorporating recycled paper, minimizing chlorine in bleaching, or recycling the energy produced at the paper mill.

This printing is printed on recycled paper containing 100% post-consumer waste.

Library of Congress Cataloging-in-Publication Data
Honeyman, Ryan.
 The B corp handbook : how to use business as a force for good / Ryan Honeyman ; foreword by the cofounders of B Lab. -- First edition.
    pages cm
 Includes bibliographical references and index.
 ISBN 978-1-62656-043-7 (pbk.)
 1. Social responsibility of business. 2. Social entrepreneurship. I. Title.
 HD60.H655 2014
 658.4'08--dc23
                          2014024911

First Edition
19 18 17 16 15 14   10 9 8 7 6 5 4 3 2 1

Cover Design: Jerrod Modica, B Lab
Interior design and composition: Seventeenth Street Studios
Illustration: Jerrod Modica, B Lab
Proofreader: Laurie Dunne
Indexer: Richard Evans
Photo credits: see page 203

To the B Corp Community

Contents

B Corps in Their Own Words

One of the most powerful aspects of this book is the opportunity to hear directly from the B Corp community—in its own words—about the benefits, challenges, and surprises of becoming a Certified B Corporation. Within this handbook you will find twenty B Corp Q&As with CEOs, executives, impact investors, and others from the following companies:

Mandy Cabot, CEO, Dansko (page 17)
Footwear—Pennsylvania

John Replogle, CEO, Seventh Generation (page 23)
Home products—Vermont

Rob Michalak, Global Director of Social Mission, Ben & Jerry's (page 27)
Ice cream—Vermont

patagonia

Rick Ridgeway, Vice President of Environmental Initiatives, Patagonia (page 34)
Outdoor apparel—California

Etsy

Matt Stinchcomb, Vice President of Values and Impact, Etsy (page 38)
E-commerce marketplace—New York

Gonzalo Muñoz, CEO, TriCiclos (page 42)
Recycling—Chile

Tiffany Jana, CEO, TMI Consulting (page 51)
Diversity and inclusion consulting—Virginia

JUHUDI KILIMO

Nat Robinson, CEO, Juhudi Kilimo (page 64)
Asset-based financing and training—Kenya

Kim Coupounas, Cofounder, GoLite (page 78)
Outdoor apparel—Colorado

Edward Perry, Cofounder and Managing Director, COOK Trading (page 82)

Frozen ready meals—United Kingdom

Tom Payne, Marketing Director, King Arthur Flour (page 88)

Baking goods—Vermont

Terence Jeyaretnam, Executive Director, Net Balance (page 100)

Sustainability consulting—Australia

Kenyatta Brame, Chief Administrative Officer, Cascade Engineering (page 104)

Manufacturing—Michigan

Tim Masson, CEO, The Ian Martin Group (page 115)

Recruitment and human resources consulting —Canada

Maria Kingery, Cofounder and CEO, Southern Energy Management (page 128)

Solar energy—North Carolina

Anders Ferguson, Partner, Veris Wealth Partners (page 134)

Impact investing—New York

Tim Frick, Principal, Mightybytes (page 144)

Web and media services—Illinois

Kevin Trapani, CEO, The Redwoods Group (page 148)

Insurance services—North Carolina

Jed Davis, Director of Sustainability, Cabot Creamery (page 160)

Dairy products—Vermont

Jenn Vervier, Director of Strategy and Sustainability, New Belgium Brewing Company (page 166)

Craft brewed beer and ales—Colorado

FOREWORD

Ryan Honeyman is a champion for a better way to do business.
Let's be honest. Sustainability consultants don't get on magazine covers.
They don't usually get to do keynotes at big conferences. The job of a sustainability consultant is to make other people look good. Kind of like a point guard in basketball.

As partners and investors in AND 1—a basketball footwear and apparel company that made a name for itself with trash talk T-shirts, baggy shorts, cool shoes, and "No he didn't!" streetball videos in the decade-plus from 1993 to 2005—we know point guards. Some point guards are famous in their own right, but the vast majority exist to make it easier for others to perform at a high level.

Ryan Honeyman is a point guard for sustainability. And although he may not help you win the adulation of the crowds, with *The B Corp Handbook* Ryan has made it easier for you to earn the admiration of your kids and your grandkids.

How do we know this to be true? It's simple: Your kids and your grandkids will demand more from work than a paycheck. They will demand a purpose. They will demand more from business than products that are made cheap, fast, and disposable. They will demand products and services that create a positive impact in the world.

As you'll read in this book, according to Goldman Sachs, this is already true among millennials, who comprise about 50 percent of the world's workforce. Yes, you read that correctly: 50 percent. Millennials want a job that offers them an opportunity to create meaning, not just make money. And those millennials are also your customers and, soon, your investors.

So this book is not for everybody. It's only for those business leaders who want to attract and retain the best talent. It's only for those marketing professionals who want to turn their customers into evangelists. It's only for those CEOs who want to attract the kind of capital that will let them build a great business for the long term. It's only for business school students and young entrepreneurs and intrapreneurs who want an easy-to-use tool kit to help them seize a big market opportunity and to bring their whole selves to work every day.

We are witnessing one of the most important cultural shifts of our time. We are in the midst of the evolution of capitalism from a century focused on maximizing short-term shareholder value to one focused on maximizing long-term shared value.

According to the largest public pension fund in the United States, CalPERS, which has $265 billion in assets under management, the companies that will create the most long-term shareholder value will be those that effectively manage their financial capital, their physical capital, and their human capital for the long term.[1] That's investor-speak for the triple bottom line: people, planet, and profit. *The B Corp Handbook* will help you do that.

Business leaders are the rock stars of our time. But the rock stars of the next generation will be different from the rock stars of today. These rock stars will build companies that are both high growth and high impact. These rock stars will make money and make a difference—at the same time. *The B Corp Handbook* will help you do that.

Like the B Corp movement itself, *The B Corp Handbook* doesn't tell you what you need to do to be a better business. It helps to make certain that you're asking the right questions, which only you can answer: Does our business serve a higher purpose? Where are the opportunities unique to our business? What practices can we implement that would create a business that is better for our workers, better for our community, better for the environment, and better for our bottom line?

Every winning team is blessed with a player that makes everyone else better. In the game of business, especially as it will need to be played to win in the years to come, Ryan Honeyman is that kind of player.

Ryan has helped a wide variety of businesses (including natural foods companies, cleaning companies, hybrid auto repair garages, and even a funeral home) go through the B Corp certification process, and he's helped some of the larger B Corps, such as Ben & Jerry's and Klean Kanteen, improve the social and environmental performance of their supply chains.

When Ryan heard that B Lab had said "Not yet" to a request to write a book about the B Corp movement, Ryan took it upon himself to write *The B Corp Handbook*. And like a true champion, Ryan recognized that the light needed to shine on others. So throughout this book you'll get to hear from a number of B Corp CEOs and marketing, human resources, and sustainability executives, in their own words, about how they're using their businesses as a force for good and why they became B Corps.

The three of us—college friends and business partners for the past twenty years—left our first careers as an entrepreneur, an operator, and an investor and decided that the highest and best use of our talents was to work together to help others use the power of business as a force for good. After years in conversation with hundreds of business leaders, we cofounded a nonprofit called B Lab that is the organizing force behind the B Corp movement.

In a relatively short time, B Lab has certified more than one thousand companies, and those Certified B Corps have worked together to pass laws in more than twenty-five U.S. states to support a better way to do business. They have also worked together to develop and promote standards for measuring, benchmarking, and improving a company's impact, standards which are being used by more than fifteen thousand businesses from thirty countries and more than one hundred global investment funds and institutional investors, from the Inter-American Development Bank, JPMorgan, Prudential, and UBS to leading community banks, credit unions, and impact investors.

That's the real power of this book—it gives you tools and tips to join these fifteen thousand businesses. Maybe you'll be inspired to become a Certified B Corp and be recognized as a leader, maybe you won't. But we hope that you'll be inspired to use your business as a force for good and that this book will help you take the next steps on that journey.

We have been privileged to watch a community form around a simple idea: to redefine success in business. We are firm believers in the African proverb that says, "If you want to go fast, go alone. If you want to go further, go together."

Use this book. Find the wisdom in the experiences of the B Corps that speaks to you, and join us.

Let's go further together.

Jay Coen Gilbert, Bart Houlahan, and Andrew Kassoy
Cofounders, B Lab

INTRODUCTION

I first found out about B Corporations while baking cookies. The flour I was using—King Arthur's unbleached all-purpose flour—had a Certified B Corporation logo on the side of the package. "That seems silly," I thought. "Wouldn't you want to be an A Corporation and not a B Corporation?" The carton of eggs I was using was rated AA. I was obviously missing something.

An online search revealed that the B logo was not a scarlet letter for second-rate baking products. B Corporations, I found, were part of a dynamic and exciting movement to redefine success in business by using their innovation, speed, and capacity for growth not only to make money but also to help alleviate poverty, build stronger communities, restore the environment, and inspire us to work for a higher purpose. The B stands for "benefit," and as a community, B Corporations want to build a new sector of the economy in which the race to the top isn't to be the best *in* the world but to be the best *for* the world.

Since my cookie-inspired discovery, I have watched the B Corp movement grow rapidly and globally. In addition to King Arthur Flour, big-name B Corps include companies like Ben & Jerry's, Cabot Creamery, Dansko, Etsy, Method, Patagonia, and Seventh Generation. There are now Certified B Corporations in more than thirty countries around the globe, including Afghanistan, Australia, Brazil, Chile, Kenya, and Mongolia (to name a few). Thought leaders such as former president Bill Clinton and Robert Shiller, the winner of the 2013 Nobel Prize in Economics, have taken an interest in the B Corp movement. *Inc.* magazine has called B Corp certification "the highest standard for socially responsible businesses," and the *New York Times* has said, "B Corp provides what is lacking elsewhere: proof."[1]

> *You ought to look at these B Corporations. . . . We've got to get back to a stakeholder society that doesn't give one class of stakeholders an inordinate advantage over others.*
>
> Bill Clinton, former president of the United States

> *I think B Corporations will make more profits than other types of companies.*
>
> Robert Shiller, Nobel laureate in economics

MEET SOME OF THE B CORPS. More than 1,000 B Corps are leading a global movement to redefine success in business.

In a time of unfortunate political gridlock, the B Corporation is an idea that has generated incredible bipartisan support. In the United States, legislation to create benefit corporations—a new corporate structure based on the B Corp idea—has been passed in "red" states like Louisiana and South Carolina, "blue" states like California and New York, swing states like Colorado and Pennsylvania, and even in Delaware, the home of corporate law, where more than 63 percent of the Fortune 500 are incorporated. It is not hard to see why this idea receives strong bipartisan support. B Corps are pro-business, pro-environment, pro-market, and pro-community.

I decided to write this book because in my work as a sustainability consultant I have found that many business owners and CEOs are intrigued and excited by the idea of B Corporations, but until now there has been no single step-by-step resource that could explain the what, why, and how of the B Corp movement. Accordingly, the first two sections of this book will outline the business case for using your business as a force for good, offer a brief history of the B Corp movement, provide a description of what B Corps are and why they are important, and highlight ten benefits of becoming a B Corp.

The third section describes the B Impact Assessment, a comprehensive tool that helps turn the desire to use business as a force for good into a series of concrete, measurable, and actionable steps.[2] This section is a great resource, whether you want to become a Certified B Corporation or you are unsure about becoming a B Corp but want a free tool to assess, compare, and implement improvements that are good for workers, good for the environment, good for communities, good for the long term, and good to the core. Whichever path you choose, this section will give you the insight, resources, and best practices necessary to make the most of your efforts.

For those who are fired up and ready to go, the Quick Start Guide in the final section outlines a six-week, step-by-step action plan to help you move forward on your journey as efficiently as possible. Like the section on the B Impact Assessment, the Quick Start Guide is designed to be useful both for businesses that want to become a Certified B Corporation and for companies that are interested in improving their social and environmental performance but are not necessarily interested in formally certifying as a B Corporation.

Most importantly, I made sure to tap into the collective wisdom of the B Corp community to help me write this book. I interviewed more than one hundred CEOs, sustainability directors, impact investors, marketing executives, human resources directors, and others from an international cohort of Certified B Corporations. The goal of these interviews was to get a wide range of opinions—directly from the B Corp community—about the business benefits of B Corp certification and the challenges that typically arise during the certification process. I also asked them to provide advice for companies that are considering whether to certify. In fact, one of the most powerful aspects of this book is the opportunity to hear fellow business leaders describe, in their own words, why their company became a B Corp and why they think B Corps matter.

In addition, you'll find that my website has downloads on a range of business, management, and leadership topics about which B Corps have something particularly useful to share. Topics include organizational strategy, creating a culture of innovation, attracting investment capital, legal considerations, and the latest tips on effective branding and marketing.[3]

There are two final things that I want you to know. First, B Corp offers a framework that any company in any state or country in the world can use to build a better business. This framework is relevant whether you are a B2B or B2C business, a local sole proprietor or a global brand, a start-up or a third-generation family business, a limited liability company or a partnership, an employee-owned company or a cooperative, a C corporation or an S corporation, or even if you are still deciding on the right structure for a new business.

Second, B Corp is relevant to you personally, whether you are attracted or repelled by such terms as *green, socially responsible,* or *sustainable*; whether you consider yourself conservative or progressive; whether you are a student, a young entrepreneur, or an experienced businessperson. If you have ever thought about how you could make a living *and* make a difference, about your legacy and the example you set for your kids, or about leading a purpose-driven life—and especially if you've thought about how you could use business as a force for good—the B Corp movement is for you.

Welcome to the future of business. Let's get started.

Ryan Honeyman
San Francisco

A Note about Certified B Corporations and Benefit Corporations

The main focus of this book is the Certified B Corporation, also referred to as a B Corp, not the U.S. legal entity known as a benefit corporation. This book prioritizes the Certified B Corporation because this certification is available to any business in the world, regardless of its existing legal structure or location of incorporation, making it the most relevant aspect of the B Corp movement for the majority of readers. Additional detail about the similarities and differences between Certified B Corporations and benefit corporations is available in the appendix.

1

Overview

Using Business as a Force for Good Is Good for Business

Before launching into the main content of this book, it is important to get one thing clear from the start: using business as a force for good is good for business. One of the most persuasive arguments for increasing your company's social and environmental performance is that you will save money, enhance profitability, and generate more business value. If you or others in your company, such as the CEO, CFO, or an influential board member, are skeptical about anything that hints of "green" or "socially responsible," then this section will give you a brief snapshot of the bottom-line, business case for sustainability.

Indeed, a veritable who's who of thought leaders such as Accenture, Deloitte, Goldman Sachs, Harvard Business School, McKinsey & Company, and PricewaterhouseCoopers have released data-driven case studies, global surveys, and exhaustive reports that offer compelling proof that using business as a force for good is good for business.

For example, Goldman Sachs reported that "more capital is now focused on sustainable business models, and the market is rewarding leaders and new entrants in a way that could scarcely have been predicted even fifteen years ago."[1] Goldman Sachs found that there has been a dramatic increase in the number of investors seeking to incorporate sustainability and environmental, social, and governance factors into their portfolio construction.

In a report that echoes this sentiment, the International Finance Corporation found that the Dow Jones Sustainability Index performed an average of 36.1 percent better than the traditional Dow Jones Index over a period of five years.[2] Comparable results have been found by some of the top academic institutions in the world. For example, a recent Harvard Business School study concluded that "high sustainability companies significantly outperform their counterparts over the long term, both in terms of stock market as well as accounting performance."[3]

Accenture, in a global study of CEOs' perspectives on sustainability, found that 93 percent of CEOs see sustainability as important to their company's future success. Accenture reported that "demonstrating a visible and authentic commitment to sustainability is especially important . . . to regain and build trust from the public and other key stakeholders, such as consumers and governments—trust that was shaken by the recent global financial crisis."[4]

Although some claim that sustainability is a passing trend, Deloitte stated that "sustainability is a critical business issue that is quickly becoming a mandatory requirement."[5] Deloitte went on to argue that social and environmental responsibility will continue to be relevant because, unlike other business issues, sustainability is being shaped by constituencies such as shareholders, regulators, consumers and customers, nongovernment organizations, and other drivers outside of a company's locus of control.

If you are on the fence, PricewaterhouseCoopers found a "positive, statistically significant, linear association between sustainability and corporate financial performance,"[6] and McKinsey, in no uncertain terms, said, "The choice for companies today is not if, but *how* they should manage their sustainability activities." McKinsey also reported that a fragmented, reactive approach to sustainability is no longer enough. "Companies can choose to see this agenda as a necessary evil—a matter of compliance or a risk to be managed while they get on with the business of business—or they can think of it as a novel way to open up new business opportunities while creating value for society."[7]

Importantly, sustainability is not just about reducing your environmental footprint. Goldman Sachs notes that "research at both the corporate and university levels suggests that this next generation of employees and consumers have specific needs at work that are dramatically different from previous generations. High among these is a desire to align personal and corporate values. To attract and retain this group, we believe that companies need to provide rewards beyond financial gain."[8]

A Brief History: From AND 1 to B Corps

I first discovered the AND 1 mixtapes in the late 1990s. The mixtapes were a series of basketball "streetballing" videos, created by the popular basketball shoe and apparel company AND 1, that featured lightning-quick ball handling, acrobatic slam dunks, and jaw-dropping displays of individual talent. I was a huge fan of the AND 1 mixtapes because the players used flashy, show-off moves that were very different from the more traditional style of basketball played in college or the NBA at the time. I was so fascinated with the mixtapes that I even integrated them into my lesson plans when I worked as an English teacher in Zhejiang Province, China.

Many years later, I was quite surprised to find out that two of AND 1's cofounders, Jay Coen Gilbert and Bart Houlahan, along with Andrew Kassoy, their longtime friend and former Wall Street private equity investor, were the people who created the Certified B Corporation (also referred to as just B Corporation, or B Corp). I learned that Gilbert's and Houlahan's experiences at AND 1, and Kassoy's on Wall Street, were central to their decision to get together to start B Lab, the nonprofit behind the B Corp movement.

AND 1 was a socially responsible business before the concept was well known, although AND 1 would not have identified with the term back then. AND 1's shoes weren't organic, local, or made from recycled tires, but the company had a basketball court at the office, on-site yoga classes, great parental leave benefits, and widely shared ownership of the company, and each year it gave 5 percent of its profits to local charities promoting high-quality urban education and youth leadership development. AND 1 also worked with its overseas factories to implement a best-in-class supplier code of conduct to ensure worker health and safety, fair wages, and professional development.

That was quite progressive for a basketball shoe company, especially because its target consumer was teenage basketball players, not conscious consumers with a large amount of disposable income. AND 1 was a company where an employee would be happy and proud to work.

AND 1 was also successful financially. From a bootstrapped start-up in 1993 to modest revenues of $4 million in 1995, the company grew to more than $250 million in U.S. revenues by 2001. This meant that AND 1—in less than ten years—had risen to become the number two basketball shoe brand in the United States (behind Nike). As with many endeavors, however, success brought its own set of challenges.

AND 1 had taken on external investors in 1999. At the same time, the retail footwear and clothing industry was consolidating, which put pressure on AND 1's margins. To make matters worse, Nike decided to put AND 1 in its crosshairs at its annual global sales meeting, in order to gain a larger share of the market. Not surprisingly, this combination of external forces and some internal miscues led to a dip in sales and AND 1's first-ever round of employee layoffs. After painfully getting the business back on track and considering their various options, Gilbert, Houlahan, and their partners decided to put the company up for sale in 2005.

HOW IT ALL STARTED. The seeds of the B Corp movement were planted at a basketball company called AND 1.

The results of the sale were immediate and difficult for Gilbert and Houlahan to watch. Although the partners went into the sale process with eyes wide open, it was still heartbreaking for them to see all of the company's preexisting commitments to its employees, overseas workers, and local community stripped away within a few months of the sale.

The Search for "What's Next?"

In their journey from basketball (and Wall Street) to B Corps, Gilbert, Houlahan, and Kassoy had a general sense of what they wanted to do next: the most good for as many people as possible for as long as possible. How this would manifest, however, was not initially clear.

Kassoy was increasingly inspired by his work with social entrepreneurs as a board member of Echoing Green (a venture capital firm focused on social change) and the Freelancers Insurance Company (a future Certified B Corporation). Houlahan became inspired to develop best practices to support values-driven businesses that were seeking to raise capital, grow, and hold onto their socially and environmentally responsible missions. And Gilbert, though proud of AND 1's culture and practices, wanted to go much further, inspired by the stories of iconic socially responsible brands such as Ben & Jerry's, Newman's Own, and Patagonia, whose organizing principle seemed to be how to use business for good.

The three friends' initial, instinctive answer to the "What's next?" question was to create a new company. Although AND 1 had a lot to be proud of, they reasoned, the company hadn't been started with a specific intention to benefit society. What if they started a company with that intention? After discussing different approaches, however, Gilbert, Houlahan, and Kassoy decided that they would be lucky to create a business as good as those created by existing social entrepreneurs such as Ahmed and Reem Rahim from Numi Organic Tea and Mike Hannigan and Sean Marx from Give Something Back Office Supplies. And more importantly, they decided that even if they could create such a business, one more business, no matter how big and effective, wouldn't make a dent in addressing the world's most pressing challenges.

They then thought about creating a social investment fund. Why build one company, they reasoned, when you could help build a dozen? That idea was also short lived. The three decided that even if they could be as effective as existing social venture funds such as Renewal Funds, RSF Social Finance, or SJF Ventures, a dozen fast-growing, innovative companies was still not adequate to address society's challenges on a large scale.

What Gilbert, Houlahan, and Kassoy realized, after speaking with hundreds of entrepreneurs, investors, and thought leaders, was that there was a need for two basic pieces of infrastructure to accelerate the growth of—and amplify the voice of—the entire socially and environmentally responsible business sector. This existing community of leaders said they needed a legal framework to help them grow while maintaining their original mission and values, and credible standards to help them distinguish their businesses in a crowded marketplace, where everyone seemed to be making claims that they were a "good" company.

To that end, in 2006 Gilbert, Houlahan, and Kassoy cofounded B Lab, a nonprofit organization dedicated to harnessing the power of business to solve social and environmental problems. The B Lab team worked with many of these leading businesses, investors, and attorneys to create a comprehensive set of performance and legal requirements, and they started certifying the first B Corporations in 2007.

B Corps: The Quick and Dirty

Certified B Corporations are companies that have been certified by the nonprofit B Lab to have met rigorous standards of social and environmental performance, accountability, and transparency. B Corp certification is similar to LEED certification for green buildings, Fair Trade certification for coffee, or USDA Organic certification for milk. A key difference, however, is that B Corp certification evaluates an entire company (e.g., worker engagement, community involvement, environmental footprint, and governance structure) rather than looking at just one aspect of a company (e.g., the building or a product). This big picture evaluation is important because it helps distinguish between good companies and just good marketing.

Today, there is a growing, global community of more than 1,000 Certified B Corporations across dozens of industries working together toward one unifying goal:

A CERTIFICATION FOR THE ENTIRE COMPANY. B Corp certification helps consumers, investors, the media, and policy makers support organizations that are using business as a force for good.

to redefine success in business so that one day all companies will compete not just to be the best *in* the world but also to be the best *for* the world.

Why B Corps Matter

Business is, for better or worse, one of the most powerful forces on the planet. At its best, business encourages collaboration, innovation, and mutual well-being, and helps people to live more vibrant and fulfilling lives. At its worst, business— and the tendency to focus on maximizing short-term profits—can lead to significant social and environmental damage, such as the BP Deepwater Horizon oil spill or the loss of more than $1 trillion in global wealth in the 2008 financial crisis.

Governments and nonprofits, moreover, are necessary yet insufficient to address society's greatest challenges. Government budgets are already constrained and are likely to be more constrained in the future, and nonprofits, for all the great work that they do, are structurally limited in their ability to attract and retain talent, to rapidly grow to meet demand, and to adapt to new challenges, because they are heavily dependent on charitable funding.

Over the past thirty years, there has been a tremendous growth in the number of conscious consumers, socially responsible investments, and triple bottom line businesses that believe that business should strive to do no harm. More recently, there also has been a chorus of voices from thought leaders such as Sir Richard Branson, Thomas Friedman, Bill Gates, and Michael Porter, who have recognized a growing trend among entrepreneurs and business leaders toward creating market-based solutions to our most pressing global challenges.

How do B Corporations fit into this bigger context? What is the point? Why do B Corps matter? There are many reasons why B Corps matter, but the following are some of the reasons that are most meaningful to me and to the hundreds of B Corp representatives I spoke to during the writing of this book.

B Corps matter because they accelerate the evolution of capitalism. Many businesses tend to focus on short-term profits, not because these businesses are inherently greedy or evil but because short-term profits are the metric that is most often measured and rewarded. B Corporations believe that capitalism needs to evolve from a twentieth-century model that heavily emphasizes short-term profits for shareholders to a twenty-first-century model that creates shared and enduring prosperity for all stakeholders (including workers, suppliers, the community, the environment, and shareholders). B Corps accelerate this existing trend by creating, using, and promoting new legal structures that aim to create value for all stakeholders, as well as transparent, credible, comprehensive, and independent

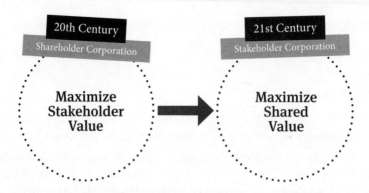

THE EVOLUTION OF CAPITALISM. B Corporations are changing the default operating system of capitalism.

third-party standards of social and environmental performance that create a more efficient and effective marketplace.

B Corps matter because they redefine success in business. B Corps create a new narrative, a new set of expectations, and a new focus on using the power of business for more than just profits. A great example of this is the work of Adam Lowry and Eric Ryan, the cofounders of Method. Lowry and Ryan took an uninspiring product category—soap—and built a movement around stylish, eco-friendly products that make cleaning safe and fun. Method's products prevent triclosan, brominated vegetable oil, sodium lauryl sulfate, and other unpronounceable ingredients from getting into our homes and the environment. Method has built an imaginative, irreverent culture that allows its employees to express themselves through their work. It has generated great returns for its investors through its mission-aligned sale to Ecover, a European home products company, and now Ecover is considering whether to become a founding European Certified B Corporation. This is a laudable—perhaps heroic—achievement. And Lowry and Ryan are not alone. There are thousands of others like them, creating businesses that are high growth and high impact.

> [B Corporations are] a powerful, no-cost, market-based solution to the systemic problem of "short-termism" and an innovative approach to using market forces to solve our most challenging problems.
>
> Jack Markell, governor of Delaware

B Corps matter because they are concrete and measurable. B Corp certification turns the ambiguous concepts of "going green" or "being a good corporate.

MAKING MONEY AND A DIFFERENCE. Method's cofounders, Adam Lowry and Eric Ryan, have created a business that is both highly profitable and highly beneficial for society and the environment.

citizen" into something tangible and measurable that people can easily identify, trust, and support. B Corps meet rigorous independent standards of performance for worker treatment, engage in their communities, and steward our environment. Most importantly, these standards—and information about how other B Corps perform against them—are transparent. This can help your business stand out in a crowded market, attract the best talent, and turn your customers into evangelists.

B Corps matter because they build collective voice. Many movements—from clean tech, microfinance, and sustainable agriculture to the Buy Local and co-op movements—are manifestations of the same idea: how to use business for good. The B Corporation amplifies the voice of this diverse marketplace behind the power of a unifying brand that stands for a better way to do business. Certified B Corporations include more than a thousand businesses, from more than sixty industries and thirty countries, that can speak with one voice when they collectively invite their thirty million closest family, friends, and followers to join them in celebrating the use of business as a force for good.

> B Corp certification helps raise awareness around what is being done well in Afghanistan. It sets an example that an Afghan company can achieve international standards for ethical operations and transparency. It also benefits other Afghan companies by opening up more mentoring opportunities and demonstrating the path to apply for B Corp certification.

Luisa Walmsley, Corporate Social Responsibility Program Manager, Roshan
TELECOMMUNICATIONS—AFGHANISTAN

B Corps matter because they are better businesses. Many business owners have told me that B Corp certification has helped them become a better business on many different levels—from attracting talent, to raising capital, to winning new business. Indeed, Certified B Corporations were 63 percent more likely to survive the Great Recession (2007–2009) than the average U.S. small business. And when B Corps survive, they benefit all of their stakeholders by creating social, environmental, and financial value.

B Corps matter because they help us live to a higher purpose. There's a reason why Rick Warren's *The Purpose-Driven Life* is among the best-selling books of all time.[9] Most people are motivated by a higher purpose, not profit. A *Huffington Post* blog by B Lab cofounder Gilbert summed up how B Corps tap into this energy: "Whether by law or custom, we believe and act as though business can have no purpose other than the maximization of profits. This belief . . . constrains our imagination and ability to live to our full potential as human beings. A full life is a life of service to something more than oneself, whether that something be family, friends, community, the environment, society, or future generations."[10]

B Corps matter because they stand for something, not against anything. The B Corp movement stands for positive, innovative, and practical solutions to global problems. There are no furious tirades about politicians or corporate greed. Indeed, on its list of core values, B Lab says, "We stand for something, not against anything." This positive, can-do philosophy is deeply appealing to me as a business owner, and I think it appeals to many other founders, investors, and executives as well.

In sum, B Corps matter because they are leading a global movement to redefine success in business, so that society will enjoy a more durable shared prosperity. As a result, we will make progress toward alleviating poverty, building stronger communities, creating great places to work, and restoring the environment, for generations to come.

A good certification may help set us apart from our competitors, but the most powerful and transformative certifications focus on bringing us all together.

Rebecca Hamilton, Director of Product Development, W.S. Badger Company
BODY AND PERSONAL CARE PRODUCTS—NEW HAMPSHIRE

Mandy Cabot, CEO
Dansko
FOOTWEAR–PENNSYLVANIA

Q: What business benefits do you directly attribute to your B Corp certification?

A: B Corp certification helps us stay focused on best practices—less operational waste, lower energy usage, a better and more complete employee handbook and sourcing code of ethics, and so on. If you really want to toe the triple bottom line, you need to hire an entire team of people to stay on top of everything. The folks at B Lab who give this their undivided attention and who can see the "all of it" do this for us, coming up with both the standards and easy-to-follow steps for improvement.

In addition, B Corps love to share. Whether it's great ideas about marketing, operations, community outreach, or sourcing, or offering discounts to fellow B Corps on goods and services, the community of B Corps generates a tremendous amount of collective goodwill, energy, and value.

Q: What advice do you have for a business that is considering B Corp certification?

A: Start by taking the assessment, even if you're unsure about becoming certified. It will likely show you things you hadn't thought of and allow you to compare your results to those of thousands of other companies. Also, involve as many people as you can in the process. If you want your values to stay top-of-mind in all your operations, involve every department in the responses. Engage non-managers as well. Give them an opportunity to lead and to offer solutions; turn them into champions and heroes.

2

Ten Benefits of
Becoming a B Corp

Typical Outcomes
for You and Your Business

In addition to B Corps' importance to the big picture, there are ten benefits to becoming a Certified B Corporation that relate more directly to you and your business. For example, B Corp certification sets you apart as a thought leader, distinguishes your business in a crowded market, and helps associate your brand with some of the most socially and environmentally responsible companies on the planet. The particular benefits that are most attractive to you will vary depending on your industry, your goals and objectives, and where you are in the life cycle of your business (e.g., whether you are seeking capital, entering a new market, or planning for succession).

I was most attracted to the quality of the community. When I found out that Dansko, King Arthur Flour, Method, and Seventh Generation were Certified B Corporations, I had no doubt that I also was going to certify my company. I had found a group of like-minded, innovative, and dynamic entrepreneurs who shared my core values. I had found my "tribe."

> *For me, the biggest surprise in our long association with the B Corp community has been the extraordinary value of our network of fellow B Corps and B Corp executives. The quality of that network has always been remarkable, and it has tangibly improved over time. We're proud to be part of it.*
>
> Bryan Welch, Publisher and Editorial Director, Ogden Publications
> *MOTHER EARTH NEWS, UTNE READER*—KANSAS

Whereas I was most attracted to the community, a consumer products company like Ben & Jerry's, Numi Organic Tea, or Preserve might find the marketing benefits to be the most valuable. This might include placing the Certified B Corporation logo on product packaging, participating in the B Corp ad campaign, or taking advantage of in-store retail partnerships. Other businesses might want to take advantage of the discounts offered to B Corps by companies such as Intuit,

MY TRIBE. Mandy Cabot, CEO of Dansko, and Bryan Welch, Publisher and Editorial Director at Ogden Publications, epitomize the genuine caring and mutually supportive spirit of the B Corp community.

NetSuite, or Salesforce. Patagonia was most attracted to the idea of protecting its social and environmental mission after its founder, Yvon Chouinard, and his wife, Malinda, retired. It really depends on your situation.

The following section describes the ten benefits that the majority of B Corps cited as the most valuable. However, these benefits are not ranked in any particular order, so feel free to start with what seems most interesting and valuable to you.

- Being part of a community of leaders with shared values
- Attracting talent and engaging employees
- Increasing credibility and building trust
- Generating press
- Benchmarking and improving performance
- Attracting investors
- Protecting a company's mission for the long term
- Building collective voice
- Saving money
- Leading a global movement

Being Part of a Community of Leaders with Shared Values

The incredible value of the community itself came as a surprise for many B Corps. Many said that they were originally interested in becoming a Certified B Corporation in order to take advantage of the marketing benefits, to receive discounts on

HIGH-FIVING FOR GOOD. Jay Coen Gilbert, cofounder of B Lab, high-fives the winners of the B Corp Champion awards at the 2012 B Corp Champions Retreat.

products and services, or to benchmark their social and environmental performance. But, almost universally, it has been the strength of the community—and the sense of being part of something bigger than an individual business—that has become the most deeply fulfilling aspect of B Corp certification.

The positivity, collaboration, excitement, innovation, and pure joy of being part of a community that shares your core values and a clear sense of purpose is what inspires, motivates, and energizes B Corps to use their businesses as a force for good. The B Corp community benefits from a high level of trust, a high quality of intellect, and an entrepreneurial spark that is more powerful than that of any other group I have ever seen.

> *I knew the certification would be valuable by itself, but I didn't anticipate the benefits of joining this vibrant community of other leaders who are passionate about finding a new way to integrate their values with their businesses.*

> Elisa Miller-Out, CEO, Singlebrook Technology
> WEB AND MOBILE SOFTWARE—NEW YORK

In many ways, the value of the B Corp community itself makes sense. The rigor of the B Corp certification process means that it takes serious dedication to complete, which helps to filter out businesses that are not truly committed to meeting high standards of performance, accountability, and transparency. The result is a passionate, highly innovative group of some of the most socially and environmentally conscious businesses on the planet.

seventh generation™

John Replogle,
CEO, Seventh Generation
HOME PRODUCTS—VERMONT

Q: What business benefits do you directly attribute to your B Corp certification?

A: Internally, the B Corp framework helps us track our progress and hold our feet to the fire. It's a way of making sure we are progressing against the journey we set out for ourselves. We were recently rated Best for the Environment, which is given to the top 10 percent of B Corporations worldwide for positive environmental impact. This has been a huge inspiration for our company.

External, it's great to be part of a strong and like-minded network. We have conversations with other B Corporations here in Vermont—like Cabot Creamery and Ben & Jerry's—on a regular basis. We also partner with B Corps like Plum Organics to cross-promote or cross-index consumers, because we have a common customer base. We even work with B Corps in our competitive space, like Method. The B Corp certification gives us a common framework to measure ourselves and to learn from each other.

Q: What advice would you give to someone who is interested in building an employee culture like you have at Seventh Generation?

A: There is a war on talent out there. It is incredibly important to get passionate, talented people to join in unison and collaborate to be constructive engineers of the next generation of how business is run. Asking "Why?" and clearly identifying your purpose will attract the very best, brightest, and most passionate people, who will be the pioneers of twenty-first-century business enterprise. That is what the B Corp movement is all about: taking a holistic, systemic approach that really upholds and supports your values every day.

In addition, although being part of a community with shared values is highly gratifying on an emotional and intellectual level, the networking, collaboration, and partnership opportunities inherent in the B Corp community also can be highly beneficial to a company's bottom line. In the San Francisco Bay Area, for example, a group of local B Corps started a series of networking groups that are designed to cultivate relationships, increase collaboration, and generate business referrals for the benefit of group members and the larger B Corp community. Similar groups have formed in Colorado, Illinois, New York, North Carolina, Oregon, Southern California, and Vermont, with more forming all the time.

B Lab also facilitates B2B Peer Circles, which are groups of B Corps that collaborate across areas of common function, expertise, geography, and interest. B2B Peer Circles have formed around a range of topics, including employee engagement, retail partnerships, women and leadership, supply chains, raising capital, diversity, and digital marketing.

> We hadn't fully grasped what an incredible support system is built into this amazing community of B Corporations. We share and benefit from each other's wisdom and experience and networks, we brainstorm together, we build mutually beneficial partnerships in a really organic way. Every company becomes greater than the sum of its parts. It's a true alliance of a very passionate community.

> Merlin Clarke, Owner, Dogeared
> HANDCRAFTED JEWELRY–CALIFORNIA

Attracting Talent and Engaging Employees

Becoming a Certified B Corporation can help unleash the passion, initiative, and imagination of employees by connecting them with the larger meaning behind their work. Goldman Sachs found that millennials, who represent nearly 50 percent of the global workforce, "have specific needs at work that are dramatically different from previous generations. High among these is a desire to align personal and corporate values. To attract and retain this group, we believe that companies need to provide rewards beyond financial gain."[1]

Research shows that millennials are not just looking for work–life balance, which means having enough time and energy to enjoy life outside of work. They also are looking for work–life integration, which means applying themselves to something that they feel passionate about, so that they can fulfill both an economic need and a need for a higher purpose.[2] Becoming a B Corporation can help

ETSY'S HACK DAY. Employees at Etsy used the B Impact Assessment to identify ways to become a better business.

you attract, retain, and engage employees around both your company's higher purpose and the B Corp community's collective purpose—to lead a global movement to redefine success in business.

> *The B Corp certification, which hardwires economic, social, and environmental aspirations into the structure of a business, is a proof point for any company seeking to hire millennial talent.*
>
> Carrie Schave, Public Relations and Marketing Manager, ROSEN
> MARKETING CONSULTING—OREGON

B Corp certification can help you attract top MBA students. In response to student demand, the Columbia, New York University, and Yale business schools now forgive the student loans of their MBA graduates who go on to work for Certified B Corporations. Indeed, the *Wall Street Journal* explains that "more companies are touting the B Corp logo, a third-party seal of environmental and social credentials, to attract young job seekers who want an employer committed to both a social mission and the bottom line."[3]

The B Impact Assessment can also be a useful framework to help engage your team in building a strong, mission-driven company culture. This worked beautifully at Etsy. Chad Dickerson, Etsy's CEO, was proud when Etsy earned the 80 points necessary to achieve B Corp certification. Dickerson also recognized that Etsy's certification marked the beginning, not the end, of their collective work to build a better business.

To further improve Etsy's social and environmental performance, Dickerson and his executive team invited their entire workforce to drop its normal workload for a B Corp Hack Day to brainstorm ideas to raise the company's score. B Corp Hack Day produced twenty-two innovative ideas, such as creating a program to track the company's carbon footprint, empowering women to take more leadership roles, improving volunteer programs with local community organizations, and increasing employee access to art studios.[4]

Increasing Credibility and Building Trust

I remember the first time I watched Simon Sinek's "How Great Leaders Inspire Action" video. In the video, Sinek explains his theory behind consumer purchasing behavior: "People don't buy what you do; they buy *why* you do it."[5] Sinek says

TRANSPARENCY BUILDS TRUST. B Corps are trusted by consumers because they have met rigorous standards of social and environmental performance, accountability, and transparency.

that customers want to connect to the story behind your brand. For example, customers want to know about your purpose in life, why you get out of bed in the morning, and why your organization exists.

In the words of marketing guru Seth Godin, "When price and availability are no longer sufficient advantages (because everything is available and the price is no longer news), then what we are drawn to is the vulnerability and transparency that bring us together, that turn the 'other' into one of us. . . . The people you seek to lead, the people who are helping to define the next thing and the interesting frontier, these people want your humanity, not your discounts."[6]

Patagonia, one of my favorite companies, is a great example of a business that effectively explains the reasoning behind everything it does. Patagonia's mission statement is "Build the best product, cause no unnecessary harm, use business to inspire and implement solutions to the environmental crisis." This mission statement doesn't just describe what the company does (build the best product); it also explains *why* it does it (to use business to inspire and implement solutions to the environmental crisis). Like many, I have a very positive opinion of Patagonia, and I continue to buy its products, because I resonate with its story.

A good story, however, is not always the whole story. Consumers increasingly do not want the next "green" product from a "brown" company. They want to know what kind of company stands behind the product or service. B Corporation certification can help you build credibility and trust in your brand because it is an independent, rigorous, third-party standard that evaluates every aspect of your business—from how your treat your workers, to your community involvement, to your overall effect on the environment.

This is important because B Corp certification, as opposed to a more limited evaluation of a building, product, or service, gives a comprehensive snapshot of the whole company, helping to turn the ambiguous concepts of "green" or "responsible" into something concrete and measurable. The Sierra Club has recognized the Certified B Corporation logo as one of the most trustworthy eco logos on the market.

Instead of saying, "We are committed to changing the world" and people raising an eyebrow, we can say, "We are B Corp certified" and people can trust that we are a better business.

Bec McHenry, Founder, The Projection Room
PROJECT MANAGEMENT—AUSTRALIA

In addition to building consumer trust through rigorous standards, B Corp certification is powerful because it increases transparency and accountability with

NUMI ORGANIC TEA

What makes us a better company?

B Impact Report

Certified since: December 2007

Summary:	Company Score	Median Score*
Governance	8	10
Workers	21	22
Community	50	32
Environment	36	9
Overall B Score	115	80

80 out of 200 is eligible for certification
• Of all businesses that have completed the B Impact Assessment
* Median scores will not add up to overall

THE B IMPACT REPORT. As for Certified B Corporations, Numi Organic Tea's B Impact Report (a summary of their full score on the B Impact Assessment) gives consumers a glimpse into the company's social and environmental performance.

regard to your company's social and environmental performance. For example, any visitor to the B Lab website can view a simple report, similar to the nutritional label on a cereal box, that shows how each Certified B Corporation performed on the Workers, Community, Environment, and Governance sections of its assessment.[7] This report makes it easy for consumers, investors, policy makers, and the media to tell the difference between good companies and just good marketing.

Research shows that social and environmental credibility is important to the modern consumer. For example, according to Goldman Sachs, consumers identified "being socially responsible" as the factor most likely to influence brand loyalty, compared with lower price, easily available products, quality, and product prestige. Goldman Sachs also reported that 52 percent of U.S. consumers claim that they actively seek information about companies' corporate social responsibility record either "all of the time" or "sometimes." The report concluded, "As

Rob Michalak, Global Director of Social Mission, Ben & Jerry's
ICE CREAM—VERMONT

Q: How did your company sell the idea of becoming a B Corp, internally?

A: This wasn't hard to do because, essentially, we were already a de facto B Corp. Our three-part mission statement (written in 1988) and unique governance structure, set up at the time when Unilever acquired Ben & Jerry's, established an independent board of directors—which is like a full board of "benefit directors." We wanted to both support and be a part of the B Corp movement by taking the official step of certification.

Q: What business benefits do you directly attribute to your B Corp certification?

A: There's no question that people place a high value on companies that manifest a social purpose alongside economic and environmental missions. We can easily argue—and find studies that show—that people are more loyal to and will switch to supporting companies with a social purpose. The B Corp certification galvanizes public confidence in companies that achieve B Corp certification. Also, the B Corp community creates more opportunities for collaboration, benchmarking, networking—a variety of elements that can improve a company's performance and ultimate success.

Q: What advice do you have for a business that is considering B Corp certification?

A: Do it. Whether you test the assessment on your own or go for official certification, it is an enlightening process that only gives you more insight into your own business and how you can improve it.

more of the millennial generation makes a significant impact on the consumer base, we believe this trend will increase."[8]

> We are always being asked questions about the Certified B Corporation because there aren't many Mongolians who are familiar with this concept. After we answer their questions, we see their faces shine up. B Corp certification increases the level of trust in our relationships with our customers and partners—trust that is vital to the conduct of our business.

Mend-Orshikh Amartaivan, Founder, The New Media Group
MEDIA CONSULTING—MONGOLIA

Generating Press

Using the power of business to solve social and environmental problems is a positive, innovative, and compelling story that has generated, and continues to generate, a high level of media interest. B Corporations have been featured in lengthy segments on *CBS Evening News*, CNN, and *PBS NewsHour*. B Corporations also have been featured in more than two thousand articles in media outlets such as the *Atlantic*, the *Economist*, the *Guardian*, the *New York Times*, and the *Wall Street Journal*. There are even a few celebrities in the B Corp movement, such as Woody

BAKERS ON A MISSION. Greyston Bakery, a B Corp that bakes brownies for companies like Ben & Jerry's and Whole Foods Market, has drawn attention from *Forbes, The Financial Times,* Marketplace, and The TODAY Show for its pioneering open hiring program.

Harrelson, cofounder of Step Forward Paper, and Jessica Alba, cofounder of The Honest Company.

> *The B Corp community is creating a buzz and an energy for a new economy that is not seen anywhere else.*

Matt Mayer, Sustainability Strategist, Conscious Brands
SUSTAINABILITY CONSULTING—CANADA

Importantly, the larger B Corps are not the only companies getting attention from the media. In both 2012 and 2013, for example, there were more than six hundred articles written about the movement, mentioning more than two hundred B Corps. *Entrepreneur* magazine published a lengthy article that featured fifteen B Corps, saying that "B Corp status . . . has become a badge of honor."[9]

One of the primary reasons that B Corporations get a lot of press is the marketing and public relations support they receive from B Lab. B Lab nominates and acts as an advocate for B Corps to receive top honors, such as a listing among *Bloomberg Businessweek*'s Top Social Entrepreneurs, recognition from the GOOD Company Project, or inclusion in *Inc.* magazine's 500/5,000 List, an annual list of the fastest-growing private companies in the United States. In 2013, Certified B Corps represented 31 percent of *Businessweek*'s Top Social Entrepreneur honorees and 25 percent of the GOOD Company Project's finalists; twenty-three B Corps were recognized on *Inc.*'s 500/5,000 List.

In addition, B Lab has helped drive awareness and recognition of the B Corp movement by generating original, compelling, and innovative content. *Fast Company*, for example, partnered with B Lab to publish "Rockstars of the New Economy," a yearlong series featuring a dozen high-growth, high-impact B Corps such as Better World Books, Happy Family, Revolution Foods, and Warby Parker. B Lab has also created an annual Best for the World list, which recognizes those companies that score in the top 10 percent of all B Corps worldwide for positive social and environmental impact. The Best for the World list has received a significant amount of attention from media outlets such as *Bloomberg Businessweek, Forbes*, the *Guardian, Inc.*, and many others.

> *One of the benefits of becoming a B Corp is the ability to leverage press opportunities. B Corps often join to promote each other's Twitter, Facebook, and Google+ updates and to work together to pitch stories to the media.*

Annabel Adams, Media Relations Manager, HUMAN Healthy Vending
NATURAL FOOD VENDING MACHINES—CALIFORNIA

Benchmarking and Improving Performance

Many B Corps report that one of the biggest benefits of the certification process is the B Impact Assessment, a free tool that measures the social and environmental performance of the entire company on a scale of zero to 200 points. This enables any business to measure the impact of its operations on its workers, its community, and the environment; to compare itself to its industry peers; and to compete to improve its performance over time. The B Impact Assessment is particularly valuable because no matter how sustainable your business already is (or is not), you will undoubtedly find blind spots that you can address to further benefit your stakeholders.

> *Before the B Impact Assessment, we struggled with aligning our internal processes and assuring our deep-thinking team members that the company was being guided for maximum impact. Now we have a road map and partners that help us establish effective governance practices and policies. Becoming a Certified B Corp put it all together for us.*
>
> Regina Wheeler, CEO, Positive Energy Solar
> SOLAR ELECTRIC SYSTEMS—NEW MEXICO

Patagonia is a great example of a company that uses the B Impact Assessment for continuous improvement. On its initial B Corp certification, Patagonia—one of the most eco-friendly companies on the planet—scored 106 out of 200 points. Although earning only half of the points on the B Impact Assessment might seem like a poor performance, Patagonia's score was well above both the 80 points required for B Corp certification and the median score of 95 points for all Certified B Corps.

Indeed, the B Impact Assessment is designed to be tough. Rather than trying to get a perfect score on the first try (which is virtually impossible, because no company is perfect), you can use the assessment to measure your company's social and environmental performance, gain valuable insights that can help spark new ideas, and motivate your company to reach for an improved score over time.

Some B Corps, such as Ben & Jerry's and Numi Organic Tea, are going further by using the B Impact Assessment to benchmark their key suppliers. The assessment's comprehensive, rigorous, and comparable metrics helps these companies better understand both the overall impact of their supply chains and the individual performance of their various suppliers. Ben & Jerry's is interested in using the B Impact Assessment to help guide its procurement and sourcing decisions in the future.

In addition, B Corps such as The Redwoods Group, a commercial property casualty insurer based in North Carolina, use the free B Impact Assessment as a guide for their corporate social responsibility reporting. In many cases, substituting the assessment for conventional corporate social responsibility reporting can save considerable time and money.

> *Our biggest surprise, considering our one hundred percent commitment to sustainable materials and ethical labor practices, was that we did not score higher on the B Impact Assessment. It was eye opening to realize that we could still improve in many different areas of our business.*
>
> Matt Reynolds, *President and Cofounder, Indigenous Designs*
> ORGANIC, FAIR TRADE APPAREL—CALIFORNIA

Attracting Investors

B Corp certification can help you attract mission-driven or impact investors who consider social, environmental, and financial criteria in their investment decisions; mainstream investors who are primarily interested in strong financial returns; or larger companies interested in acquiring a cutting-edge and innovative brand.

For example, Plum Organics, a fast-growing organic baby food company, was sold to and is now a wholly owned subsidiary of the Campbell Soup Company.

Investors	Certified B Corps
Good Capital	Better World Books
Union Square Ventures	Etsy
Simon Equities	Method
Catterton Partners	Plum Organics
Benchmark	Farmigo
Mohr Davidow Ventures	Rally Software
Kleiner Perkins	Recycle Bank
Tiger Global Management	Warby Parker

ACCESS TO CAPITAL. A wide variety of Certified B Corps have received investment capital.

patagonia

Rick Ridgeway, Vice President of Environmental Initiatives, Patagonia

OUTDOOR APPAREL—CALIFORNIA

Q: Why did Patagonia become a Certified B Corporation?

A: The principle benefit to Patagonia from B Corp certification—that now is formalized by the new California benefit corporation law—is the mechanism it provides to protect the company's core values during succession. Another important one is how B Corp certification provides the company a quantified measurement of its performance in living up to our environmental, social, and governance values.

Q: Why do you think B Corps are important?

A: B Corp enshrines Patagonia's nearly fifty-year-old model of business into law, and that makes it easier for other businesses to adopt this model and use it in their own search for stewardship and sustainability. Our mission is to "build the best product, cause no unnecessary harm, [and] use business to inspire and implement solutions to the environmental crisis." B Corp certification provides the company an additional opportunity to measure our success against our mission.

Q: What would you tell someone considering becoming a Certified B Corp?

A: B Corp certification is a mechanism for companies not only to measure their performance but also to share those measurements with their constituents, including shareholders and customers. Patagonia believes that companies that practice full transparency will be the ones in the future rewarded most fully both by their shareholders and by their customers.

MISSION PROTECTED. Yvon Chouinard was first in line to register Patagonia as California's first benefit corporation. Patagonia then became a Certified B Corp the next day, making clear to its stakeholders that Patagonia met the highest standards of third-party-verified performance.

Rather than viewing Plum Organic's B Corp certification as an impediment, Campbell's saw the B Corp certification as a valuable asset that could help Plum retain the trust of its most loyal customers after the sale. To show its support, Campbell's helped Plum Organics register as one Delaware's first benefit corporations, when the law came into effect in August 2013.

Method's recent merger followed a similar path. Method, the quirky, B Corp-certified maker of home cleaning products, was acquired in 2013 by Ecover, a leading European cleaning company. Ecover also supported Method in registering as a Delaware benefit corporation, and now Ecover itself is considering whether to become a founding European Certified B Corporation.

As mentioned, becoming a B Corp can help a company raise capital from a wide variety of investors. For example, mainstream venture capitalists such as Kleiner Perkins Caufield & Byers, New Enterprise Associates, and Tiger Asset Management are investing in Certified B Corporations because they have found that B Corps can be great financial investments. Union Square Ventures, a venture capital firm that invested in Etsy (and has also invested in Foursquare, Twitter, and Zynga), says B Corps are appealing because the companies that produce the most stakeholder value over the next decade will also produce the best financial returns.

Our shareholders knew about and supported our B Corp certification. Harvest Power is focused on profitability as a business, and I don't think becoming a B Corporation contradicts that.

Paul Sellew, Founder and Chairman, Harvest Power
RENEWABLE ENERGY AND SOIL ENHANCEMENT—MASSACHUSETTS

Another benefit of becoming a B Corp is that all Certified B Corps receive a free Global Impact Investment Rating System (GIIRS) rating and a free listing on B Analytics, an investor-facing platform designed by B Lab. This can help your company raise money, because a large number of investors with billions of dollars of assets under management—from global financial institutions such as JPMorgan, Prudential, and UBS to leading impact investors such as Good Capital, Renewal Funds, and RSF Social Finance—prefer to invest in GIIRS-rated companies (and Certified B Corps). These investors trust rigorous, comparable, and verified social and environmental performance metrics.

In addition, B Lab can help you raise money by providing direct introductions to the many Certified B Corps in the financial services industry (including commercial banks, venture funds, asset managers, wealth advisors, and investment banks) as well as to the wide variety of funds and institutional investors that use B Lab's B Analytics platform. For example, B Lab introduced United By Blue, a B Corp–certified apparel company based in Philadelphia, to Investors' Circle, a group of local impact investors. After several meetings, Investors' Circle decided to make the largest investment in the organization's history, helping United By Blue expand its wholesale business into retail.

It's been very helpful to be able to point to our B Corp certification—and inviting potential investors to look into the B Corp methodology—as a "one-stop shop" to show how we measure our social and environmental impact.

Ben Sandzer-Bell, CEO, *CO2 Bambu*
PREFABRICATED BAMBOO HOUSING—NICARAGUA

Protecting a Company's Mission for the Long Term

One of the primary challenges that the B Corp was created to address is the difficulty that many entrepreneurs have in raising capital, growing, or selling a business without diluting the company's original social and environmental values. Therefore, Certified B Corporations, in addition to meeting rigorous standards of social and environmental performance, amend their governing documents—the legal DNA of their business—to be more supportive of maintaining their social and environmental mission over time.

This expanded legal protection for a company's mission is particularly relevant in succession planning. For example, many businesses, such as Ben & Jerry's, Burt's Bees, and Tom's of Maine, started out with charismatic, dynamic leaders who had strong social and environmental values. However, if the original founders retire, the company wants to take on new investors in order to grow, or the company is put up for sale, those strong core values could be diluted by the new CEO, investors, or owners in favor of increased short-term profits.

By becoming a B Corporation, entrepreneurs can protect their mission by elevating their company's core social and environmental values to the status of law, meaning that a new CEO and/or new investors would be obligated to consider both shareholders *and* stakeholders when making decisions in the future. This helps ensure that such a company will continue to benefit society and the environment for the long term.

This is exactly what inspired Patagonia to become a B Corporation. Yvon and Malinda Chouinard credit the B Corp legal structure—which they officially put in place when they registered Patagonia as California's first benefit corporation— with giving them the peace of mind that the environmental mission at the heart of the company's decades-long success would be safe after they retired.

Patagonia is trying to build a company that could last one hundred years. Benefit corporation legislation creates the legal framework to enable mission-driven companies like Patagonia to stay mission driven through succession, capital raises, and even changes in ownership, by institutionalizing the values, culture, processes, and high standards put in place by founding entrepreneurs.

Yvon Chouinard, Founder, Patagonia
OUTDOOR APPAREL—CALIFORNIA

Building Collective Voice

Many of the movements taking place around the globe—from clean tech, microfinance, and sustainable agriculture to the buy local and cooperative ownership movements—are manifestations of the same idea: how to use business for good. The B Corporation organizes and amplifies the voices of this diverse marketplace behind the power of a unifying brand. More than 1,000 businesses from more than sixty industries and thirty countries can now speak with one voice when

Etsy

Matt Stinchcomb,
Vice President of
Values and Impact, Etsy

E-COMMERCE MARKETPLACE—NEW YORK

Q: What business benefits do you directly attribute to your B Corp certification?

A: The most profound changes have been internal. The certification process showed us where we have tremendous opportunity to make important and high-impact improvements to our operations and culture. B Corp certification has served as a galvanizing force in our march toward mission-driven business. It was a tangible, meaningful, and important first step in our journey, and the company rallied behind it.

Q: What was your biggest surprise about becoming a B Corp?

A: We thought we were pretty progressive, and we barely passed![10]

Q: If you could change one thing about the B Corp movement, what would it be?

A: We wish we would have known about B Corps when we were first starting out. Now that we do, we want to help it become the default corporate structure for the world.

they collectively invite their millions of friends, family, and followers to join them in using business as a force for good.

This platform enables the B Corp community to build a collective voice that is more powerful than any individual company. For example, when the B Corp logo is used on fifteen million bags of King Arthur Flour, or Ben & Jerry's uses the logo in its marketing and promotional materials, or GoLite creates an entire retail store based on the B the Change campaign, it benefits more than those individual brands. These individual actions benefit the entire B Corp community by strengthening and elevating the message about a better way to do business.

Thanks to the generosity of fellow Certified B Corporation Ogden Publications, for instance, B Corp ads have appeared in *Mother Earth Living, Mother Earth News*, and *Utne Reader*, reaching more than five million conscious consumers to date. The latest version of the ad campaign encourages consumers to "Take a Deeper Look," emphasizing the transparency and third party–validated performance of Certified B Corps.

> *Our biggest surprise was that there was a world outside of our own individual commitment to being a good company. We feel accompanied and supported, whereas before we felt like soloists on this now orchestrated quest.*
>
> Juan Manuel Soto, CEO, Acción Verde
> ECOLOGICAL RESTORATION—COLOMBIA

Saving Money

Although saving money is not usually the primary motivation behind a company's decision to become a Certified B Corporation, it is definitely appreciated. B Corps have collectively enjoyed more than $5 million in savings through access to partnership discounts with organizations such as Intuit, NetSuite, and Salesforce. These partnerships were developed by B Lab. B Corporations also provide one another with hundreds of product and service discounts, such as discounts on consulting, marketing, office management, capital raising, travel, human resources, legal, design, media, and web development services.

On a municipal level, several U.S. cities have supported the B Corp movement by creating modest tax incentives and procurement preferences. The City of San Francisco, for example, passed legislation that gives benefit corporations a 4 percent discount (relative to other applicants) when bidding for more than $1 billion in city contracts. Similarly, the City of Philadelphia created a pilot

Business Case:

BetterWorldBooks®

Salesforce: Discount on yearly CRM licenses

Inspire Commerce: Discount on all credit card processing

B Corp E-Commerce Retail Package: Promotional campaign generating 500K new leads

B Corp Ad Campaign: Free ads in national magazines reaching 5 million Readers

Total Savings to Date: $300,000

BIG SAVINGS. Certified B Corps have saved more than $5 million through access to a variety of partnership discounts.

$500,000 tax break program for twenty-five Certified B Corps over five years. The Philadelphia program was enacted because B Lab has been collecting compelling data that shows that B Corps create higher-quality jobs and help support local communities.

Leading a Global Movement

B Corporations recognize that changing the world is a team sport. Whether you are a sole proprietor, a national brand, or global business with billions in sales, and whether your focus is on strengthening local communities, reducing global poverty, or addressing climate change, being part of a larger movement can help build collective voice, accelerate the adoption of standards, drive capital, pass supportive public policies, and inspire consumers to change their behavior.

A key element of creating lasting change is a vibrant, diverse, and growing community that can shift our expectations about what it means to be a good business. The B Corp movement has clearly tapped into an idea that resonates with entrepreneurs around the globe.

B Lab has partnered with several organizations to help drive the movement globally. At the 2012 Clinton Global Initiative annual meeting, for example, B Lab formally launched a partnership with Sistema B to serve and support the community of Certified B Corporations ("Empresas B") in South America.[11] The ini-

A Global Movement to use Business as a Force for Good

Canada · United Kingdom · Netherlands · Mongolia · Ireland · Belgium · France · Turkey · Afghanistan · South Korea · United States · Italy · Lebanon · Spain · Israel · Hong Kong · Mexico · Nicaragua · India · Vietnam · Guatemala · Costa Rica · Colombia · Venezuela · Kenya · Brazil · Tanzania · Peru · Australia · Chile · Argentina · New Zealand

30+ Countries

NOW WITH 25 PERCENT MORE GLOBAL. Although the B Corp movement originally started in Pennsylvania, more than 25 percent of all Certified B Corps are now based outside of the United States.

tial focus of this partnership will be on developing a community of Empresas B in Argentina, Brazil, Chile, and Colombia. As a sign of the rising popularity of the movement, the Certified B Corporation was named the number one idea on a list of one hundred ideas that could change the world, compiled by *Semana Sostenible,* a popular magazine based in Colombia.

Other exciting partnerships include the launch of B Lab Europe, the establishment of a B Lab office in Australia, and B Lab's collaboration with MaRS Discovery District to support the B Corp community in Canada.[12] In fact, the total number of Canadian B Corps grew by 65 percent in 2013.

During interviews conducted for this book, representatives of Certified B Corps from all over the world—Argentina, Brazil, Chile, Colombia, Costa Rica, Guatemala, Italy, Mexico, and Turkey, as well as Canada and the United States—repeatedly described participation in a global movement to redefine success in business as an incredibly invigorating and profound experience.

People keep saying, "Oh, you are a B Corp? That's amazing! How do you do it?" This happens at least twice a week.

Sebastian Salinas Claro, CEO, Emprediem
SOCIAL INNOVATION MANAGEMENT AND TRAINING—CHILE

TRICICLOS

Gonzalo Muñoz, CEO, TriCiclos
RECYCLING—CHILE

Q: What business benefits do you directly attribute to your B Corp certification?

A: The B Corp certification is a fantastic path that allows any business to increase their impact and their best practices. You have the opportunity to get to know many other extraordinary businesses with whom you can get involved or learn from. In addition, becoming a B Corp gives us an additional layer of credibility that helps us with new business opportunities.

Q: What was the biggest challenge you had to overcome to certify as a B Corp?

A: Our biggest challenge was increasing our level of transparency. We had very good practices but were not totally committed to showing ourselves to our stakeholders. That was challenging, and definitely worth it.

Q: What was your biggest surprise about becoming a B Corp?

A: The biggest surprise was realizing we were the first B Corp in South America. That gave us an additional strength to work on globalizing the B Corp movement.

3

The B Impact Assessment

How to Use Business as a Force for Good

The B Impact Assessment is a comprehensive tool that helps turn the idea of using business as a force for good into a series of concrete, measurable, actionable steps. Whether you want to become a Certified B Corporation or are unsure about B Corp certification but want a free tool to assess, compare, and improve your social and environmental performance, the B Impact Assessment is your starting point.

This part of the *Handbook* will help you learn how to use the B Impact Assessment efficiently and effectively. In particular, we will look more closely at how you can use your business as a force for good, we will show you a Quick Assessment worksheet that can give you a rough idea of how you might score on the B Impact Assessment, and we will ask you a few reflection questions to help you plan your next steps.

This handbook is designed to be used, not just read. Feel free to grab a pen, write in the margins, and circle, underline, and highlight as you go. Here are a few frequently asked questions to help you get started on your journey.

What Is the B Impact Assessment?

The B Impact Assessment is a free, confidential, easy-to-use online management tool that assesses your company's social and environmental performance on a 200-point scale, compares your results to thousands of businesses, and gives you access to resources and best practice guides that can help you improve your performance over time.[1]

The B Impact Assessment is designed to accommodate all types of businesses, including manufacturers, retailers, and service companies; businesses of varying size, from sole proprietorships to multinational corporations; and companies from both developed and emerging markets. The B Impact Assessment is standardized to create an even playing field among all groups. This gives any company the ability to identify where it is doing well and where it has room for improvement, whether the company is just starting out or is taking its one thousandth step on this path.

How Much Does the B Impact Assessment Cost?

The B Impact Assessment, including access to the best practice guides, comparative data, and an individualized improvement report, is a free public service provided by B Lab. If you are interested in becoming a Certified B Corporation, there is an annual B Corp certification fee.[2] Taking the B Impact Assessment does not obligate your company to become a Certified B Corporation.

Will My Data Be Confidential?

Everything you enter into the B Impact Assessment is entirely confidential. None of your company's individual answers will be shared with anyone. In order to create useful comparable metrics for benchmarking purposes, B Lab collects anonymous data from more than fifteen thousand users of the B Impact Assessment. This data is only used in aggregate and is not linked to any company's specific answers.

How Much Time Does it Take?

It takes around ninety minutes to do a quick trial run of the B Impact Assessment. The most effective strategy for first-timers taking the B Impact Assessment is to keep moving. Make ballpark estimates, skip questions you don't know the answers to, and try to complete the entire assessment in ninety minutes or less. The initial goal is to get a broad overview of the types of questions asked on the B Impact Assessment, not to attempt to answer all of the questions correctly on the first go.

The B Impact Assessment seemed daunting when we first began. Looking back, however, the process was incredibly worthwhile, and we encourage others to join us on this path.

Michael "Luni" Libes, Founder and Managing Director, Fledge
BUSINESS INCUBATION AND ACCELERATION—WASHINGTON

Who in Our Company Should Complete the Assessment?

If it is possible, at least for small and mid-sized businesses, I recommend that the CEO undertake the first round of the B Impact Assessment, because the CEO has a unique perspective on the entire company's operations, knows the strategic direction of the company, and has the power to keep the process moving internally. If it is not possible to have the CEO involved from the start, I recommend appointing an "internal champion" who is tasked with completing a first draft of the assessment and convening a supporting team to review the results. The internal champion can be anyone—the CFO or COO, your sustainability director or human resources manager, an associate, or even an intern.

Can a Start-Up Take the B Impact Assessment?

Many start-ups find that the assessment is a useful learning tool to help them create a solid, mission-driven foundation for their new businesses, and I encourage you to begin using the B Impact Assessment from day one. To become a Certified B Corporation, however, you will need to have been in operation for at least six months because B Corp certification looks at past performance rather than future intentions.

Recently, in response to demand from start-ups and the growing number of incubators and accelerators that serve them, B Lab has created a temporary "Pending Certification" status for start-ups that have been in operation for less than six months. This is a great way for entrepreneurs to build their business on a strong mission-driven foundation and benefit from being a member of the B Corp community from the start.

What Is a Good Score and What Does My Score Mean?

Any positive score indicates that the company is doing something beneficial for society and the environment. Most companies score somewhere between 40 and 60 points out of a possible 200. Companies interested in becoming a Certified B Corporation are required to score 80 points or higher. The median score for all Certified B Corps is 95.

> We were surprised at how rigorous the actual B Corp certification process was! We failed twice before eventually succeeding in our bid to become certified.
>
> Nancy Vollmer, Entrepreneur and Retail Consultant, institute B
> ENTREPRENEURSHIP INCUBATOR—CANADA

What Is the B Impact Report?

The B Impact Report is a free, one-page report that shows how your company performed on the Workers, Community, Environment, and Governance sections of the B Impact Assessment. This report can help you create a plan to improve your performance in the impact areas that matter most to you.[3]

How Does This Section of the Handbook Relate to the Online Version of the B Impact Assessment?

You will notice that the names, order, and framing of the following sections are similar to but do not exactly mimic the online version of the B Impact Assessment. For example, the five sections on the B Impact Assessment are officially called Workers, Community, Environment, Governance, and Impact Business Models. Here, the Good for Workers, Good for Communities, and Good for the Environment sections roughly mirror the official names on the B Impact Assessment. However, Good for the Long Term is the name I've given to the Governance section of the assessment, and Good to the Core is the name I've given to the Impact Business Model section. I have slightly tweaked the titles of the last two to better reflect the intention behind those sections.

In addition, not all of the questions that appear in the online version of the B Impact Assessment appear here. My goal is to help you better understand the process of taking the B Impact Assessment, to help you address some of the more difficult questions, and to give you best practice ideas on how to improve your score, not to recreate the entire assessment in paper form. The benefit of this approach is that it will make this book applicable to a wider variety of businesses and will help keep the book relevant as B Lab continues to update the B Impact Assessment over time.

How Can I Get More Help?

There are a number of ways to get help on the B Impact Assessment. Try using the Help buttons located throughout the assessment, which provide definitions and tips to help you answer each question accurately. B Lab also provides more than forty resource guides to help you implement new practices or policies.[4]

Tip: We found that fitting our business into the structured business models in the assessment was more of a challenge than anticipated. Our suggestion would be to engage B Lab early on in the process to help get clarity around this part of the assessment, if you're finding yourself facing a similar issue.

Ashley Bloom, Associate, Metropolitan Group
STRATEGY AND MARKETING—OREGON

Any Other Advice before I Start?

Remember, there is no single correct way to be a good company. You will need to choose your own path based on your core values, team interests, industry, and overall business strategy. Use the B Impact Assessment as a framework to reinforce your values, as a road map to help guide your path to achieving your mission, and as a tool to help you implement new socially and environmentally responsible business practices. It is not important where you start, only that you take the next step.

Tiffany Jana, CEO,
TMI Consulting
DIVERSITY AND INCLUSION CONSULTING—VIRGINIA

Q: What business benefits do you directly attribute to your B Corp certification?

A: Our business has grown 800 percent since becoming a Certified B Corporation. Between the public relations, expanded community, networking opportunities, and the social capital, TMI has experienced unprecedented growth.

Q: What was your biggest surprise about becoming a B Corp?

A: My biggest surprise was the social capital B Corp community membership gave me with millennials. I can barely keep up with the droves of highly qualified, passionate, values-aligned millennials who want to work for TMI. I am in the process of creating opportunities for several highly engaged millennials, and I meet more of them on a monthly basis. I no longer search for high-potential staff; they now come to me.

Q: What advice do you have for a business that is considering B Corp certification?

A: I would say it is worth researching B Corps in your industry. This is an emerging sector, so many companies have the opportunity to be leaders in helping shape best practices within their industries. Take this as a brilliant opportunity to influence your industry for the better and make the changes you think are necessary to evolve it to the next level.

Good for Workers

Why this matters: Your company wants to attract and retain the best talent, and talented people want to bring their whole selves to work every day.

Worker Ownership

Work Environment

Compensation, Benefits and Wages

Quick Assessment of Worker Impact

Want to get a quick idea of how good your company is for workers? Take the following fifteen-item Quick Assessment to measure your performance over the past year. You can add up your total at the bottom for a rough idea of how you might score on this section of the B Impact Assessment.

Check the box if you and/or your company . . .

Compensation, Benefits, and Wages

☐ pay a living wage to employees (including part-time and temporary employees) and independent contractors.

☐ review a compensation study for your industry to determine whether you are paying above-market, market, or below-market rates.

☐ determine the multiple that your highest-paid worker earns compared to your lowest-paid full-time worker.

☐ offer employees the same benefits as are given to executives and management.

☐ offer a retirement plan such as a 401(k) or pension, and/or profit sharing to all employees.

☐ offer a socially responsible investment option in your retirement plan.

☐ subsidize professional development and training for your workers.

☐ offer outplacement services and/or a severance package for terminated full-time workers.

Worker Ownership

☐ offer stock options, stock equivalents, and/or have a plan in place to transfer ownership of the company to full-time employees.

Work Environment

☐ have a health and wellness program.

☐ distribute an employee handbook.

☐ conduct regular, anonymous worker satisfaction and engagement surveys.

☐ regularly collect (and make transparent) data on employee metrics such as retention, turnover, and diversity.

☐ give employees part-time, flextime, or telecommuting options, as appropriate.

☐ have an employee committee to monitor and advise on occupational health and safety.

_____ Total

If you scored from **zero to 3,** you will have some work do to earn B Corp certification. Alternatively, you can make up ground with an outstanding performance in the other areas.

If you scored from **4 to 6**, you are a good candidate for B Corp certification, assuming you perform similarly well on the other sections.

If you scored from **7 to 15,** fantastic work! You are likely well on your way to getting the score you need for B Corp certification.

To see how your company stacks up against thousands of other businesses and for more best practice guides and resources, go to **www.bimpactassessment.net.** Don't worry; it's free and confidential.

T o be good for workers will mean different things to different people, depending on the size of your company, your industry, and your geographic location. However, many of the underlying themes are applicable to any business. For example, the benefits provided by a solar company may be different from the benefits provided by a bank, but the importance of supporting your employees is equally important in both industries.

The B Impact Assessment asks you to think about how your company treats its workers in three major areas: compensation, benefits, and training. It includes topics such as paying a living wage, offering health care benefits, and professional development; work environment, which includes employee engagement, turnover, and health and safety; and worker ownership, which looks at profit sharing, stock options, and employee ownership.

To assist you in your journey, I will highlight some of these topics, discuss why they are important, explain why they are rewarded on the assessment, and offer tips, resources, and advice to help you implement these practices at your company.

If you have not already done so, I encourage you to spend a few minutes on the Quick Assessment at the beginning of this section to help you identify areas for improvement. There is also a Reflections and Next Steps worksheet at the end of this section that can help guide your progress on the path.

✓ **Pay a living wage to employees (including part-time and temporary employees) and independent contractors. Review a compensation study for your industry to determine whether you are paying above-market, market, or below-market rates.**

Why Is This Rewarded?

Many employers understand that the minimum wage is insufficient to meet many of their employees' basic needs, such as food, housing, child care, and medical care. As a result, employers are starting to pay a "living wage," not only to attract and retain talent but also to help their workers climb out of cyclical poverty. The B Impact Assessment rewards the proactive efforts of these employers and rewards employers who implement this practice for their entire workforce.

Perhaps counterintuitively, paying your employees more (i.e., at least a living wage) is more beneficial for your business than the money you would save by paying them less. For example, Goldman Sachs found that "there is a high correlation across all sectors in terms of cash flow generated relative to payroll per employee." The report goes on to say that this finding "breaks with the common preconception of improving operational efficiency through cutting payroll and, on the contrary, seems to suggest that companies that invest in their workforce will reap exponential benefits."[5]

> Ben & Jerry's commitment to economic justice starts with our employees. We are committed to paying all of our Ben & Jerry's Vermont full-time workers a livable wage—enough to allow for a quality of life that includes decent housing, health care, transportation, food, recreation, savings, and miscellaneous expenses. Every year we recalculate the livable wage to make sure it's keeping up with the actual cost of living in Vermont. In 2013, for example, the lowest-paid hourly worker at Ben & Jerry's earned 46 percent above the living wage in our area.

Rob Michalak, Global Director of Social Mission, Ben & Jerry's
ICE CREAM—VERMONT

How Can You Implement This at Your Company?

First, find out what the living wage is for your community (i.e., the wage a full-time employee would need to support a family of four above the federal poverty line). Living wages in the United States range from $8 to $20 an hour.

Next, you will want to calculate what percentage of your employees already earns this wage (or higher). Many employers are surprised to find that most of their employees already earn above this minimum threshold. Your wages may need to be adjusted for a much smaller percentage of your workforce than originally anticipated.

If possible, try to compare your compensation rate to other businesses in your industry. Check your local trade association to see whether it has published a compensation study that you can reference.[6] You also can check the U.S. Bureau of Labor Statistics for wage averages in a variety of industries.

✓ **Determine the multiple that your highest-paid worker earns compared to your lowest-paid full-time worker. Evaluate the differences in benefits offered to executives, management, and workers.**

Why Is This Rewarded?

This question highlights the growing issue of wage disparity. For example, in 2012 the average pay ratio of a Fortune 50 CEO compared to the average salary of Fortune 50 employees was 379:1.[7] Some employers have started to implement a cap on the ratio between the highest and lowest earners in their company. Namaste Solar, for example, caps the ratio of its highest salary to its lowest salary at 3:1, and Whole Foods Market caps its highest salary at nineteen times the average employee pay. Certified B Corps that implement this practice typically cap their pay ratio between 5:1 and 10:1.

> *Restructuring the payment and perks offered to our employees, so that production workers could reap the same benefits as upper management, was an important step toward equality for every team member.*
>
> Merlin Clarke, Owner, Dogeared
> HANDCRAFTED JEWELRY—CALIFORNIA

Many businesses adopt this practice in order to build trust and unity among employees. John Mackey, co-CEO of Whole Foods Market, remarked:

> *At Whole Foods Market, everyone from the CEO to entry-level team members has the same benefits. The only differences are based on tenure with the company—the longer someone has been with the company, the greater his or her paid time off and the larger the company contribution toward health-care premiums and company-funded health-care reimbursement accounts. A cashier who has worked for the company for several years enjoys the same benefits enjoyed by the two co-CEOs of the company. It's very powerful to be able to tell people about this practice. It creates a sense of solidarity throughout the organization.*[8]

How Can You Implement This at Your Company?

For many companies, the cost of adjusting base compensation to meet a specific highest- to lowest-wage ratio will be marginal, as the changes would affect only a small number of entry-level employees. Matching benefits for both executive and nonexecutive employees, on the other hand, is probably a larger financial commitment and could instead be a long-term goal.

✓ **Offer a retirement plan such as a 401(k) or pension, and/or profit sharing to all employees, and offer a socially responsible investment option in your retirement plan.**

Why Is This Rewarded?

A key component of building a business that is good for workers is helping your employees build long-term financial security. Creating an employee retirement plan can be a smart way to attract and retain valuable employees, reduce your company's tax burden, and allow you to invest money in your own retirement.

Regardless of the type of plan you choose, consider offering your employees a socially responsible investment option. SRI funds typically screen out companies that are involved with alcohol, cigarettes, guns, or fossil fuels, as well as companies with labor, human rights, or environmental violations.

Offering an SRI fund will give your employees the choice to better align their financial investments with their personal values. If your company does not have a socially responsible fund but already funds a retirement plan, you will still receive credit on the B Impact Assessment. The SRI option is an incremental opportunity to do more good.

How Can You Implement This at Your Company?

If your company does not have a plan, setting one up is relatively inexpensive. If you already have a plan, try giving your employees an anonymous survey to see whether an SRI option would be valuable to them. The Society of Human Resource Management found that the number of SRI funds is likely to double in the next few years to match the rapidly growing interest.[9]

Next, ask your benefits administrator whether there are any SRI options available in your plan. If not, familiarize yourself with the B Corporations that have expertise in this field. For example, Green Retirement Plans and Social(k), both founding B Corporations, have partnered to create a popular SRI investing platform.

For additional information on adding socially and environmentally responsible investment options to your retirement plan, please see the Resources section in the back of the book.

✓ **Subsidize professional development and training for your workers.**

Why Is This Rewarded?

In his book *Drive*, author Daniel Pink explains that employees are motivated by three primary drives: autonomy, or the desire to direct one's own life; mastery, or the urge to get better at something that matters; and purpose, or the yearning to work in the service of something larger than oneself.[10] Providing employees with educational and/or professional development opportunities helps to challenge them and encourages them to build mastery in a particular domain. It also can help prepare them to move into management or other vacant internal positions.

How Can You Implement This at Your Company?

Zappos has tied educational and professional development opportunities to employee pay raises. Tony Hsieh, the CEO of Zappos, says that one of the biggest keys to employee happiness is the idea of "perceived control." In his book, *Delivering Happiness*, Hsieh explains:

> In our call center, we used to give raises once a year to our reps, which they didn't really have any control over. We later decided to implement a "skill sets" system instead. We have about twenty different skill sets (analogous to merit badges in the Boy Scouts), with a small bump in pay associated with each of the skill sets. It's up to each individual rep to decide whether to get trained and certified on each of the skill sets. If someone chooses not to get any, then he or she simply stays at the same pay level. If someone is ambitious and wants to gain all twenty skill sets, we let the rep decide on the right pace to achieve that. We've since found our call center reps are much happier being in control of their pay and which skill sets to attain.[11]

Zappos offers professional development courses on such topics as coaching, finance, leadership, public speaking, and time management. Zappos also has found success in offering three smaller promotions every six months, instead of one promotion every eighteen months. The end result is the same as the previous promotion schedule, in terms of training, certification, and pay. However, Hsieh says that his employees are much happier because there is an ongoing sense of perceived progress.

Before creating internal training, I recommend searching for opportunities that might already exist in your local business networks or industry groups. Many B Corps offer a training budget—typically $1,000 to $2,500 per employee—to be used at the employee's discretion, sometimes requiring a manager's approval to ensure that the training is work-related. This allows the employee to decide which professional development opportunities he or she wants to pursue (e.g., industry trade shows, conferences, or trade-specific accreditation).

✓ **Offer outplacement services and/or a severance package for terminated full-time workers.**

Why Is This Rewarded?

Not every hire works out. Even iconic businesses like Nike and Patagonia go through rough patches. Outplacement programs and severance packages are rewarded because they demonstrate a company's proactive effort to help workers who are laid off. Common outplacement services include group workshops, one-on-one coaching, and assistance with résumé writing, job search, and interview skills. Some outplacement services include office space and services for laid-off workers to use during their job search.

Severance packages, which typically are a combination of money and continuing benefits, are particularly helpful for low-wage workers, who can use this assistance to meet basic expenses for a short time while they secure another source of income.

Example: Rhino Foods

Rhino Foods, a Vermont-based Certified B Corp and manufacturer of novelty ice-cream products, is in an industry where production soars during a particular season and drops off sharply during the other. Due to the seasonal nature of its work, Rhino was continually laying off employees after its main production season and rehiring a new set of employees the following year. This model was both expensive for the company and difficult for the workers who needed to find a job for the other six months of the year. Rhino continued to research various solutions until, quite serendipitously, it found another local company that only needed employees during those other six months of the year. Rhino's workers now have year-round employment and Rhino has a cohort of well-trained employees who return every year.

How Can You Implement This at Your Company?

There are no specific rules about what constitutes a good severance package. Patagonia, for example, pays severance to nonexecutive employees who depart in good standing after two years. Patagonia's employee handbook also specifies the severance amount as a percentage of salary.

Many employers find it valuable to use a firm that specializes in outplacement services. Your benefits administrator or attorney should be able to recommend a local firm.

For additional information on offering outplacement services and/or a severance package for terminated full-time workers, please see the Resources section in the back of the book.

✓ **Offer stock options, stock equivalents, and/or transfer ownership of the company to full-time employees.**

Why Is This Rewarded?

In the United States, an employee stock ownership plan is an employee benefit plan, similar in some ways to a profit-sharing plan, through which employees acquire an increasing ownership stake in the company as they accumulate seniority. This practice is rewarded because ESOPs can assist in fostering employee morale, improving employee productivity, and attracting and retaining talent.

In addition, ESOPs present an opportunity to reduce your company's income taxes significantly. Depending on your corporate structure, the percentage of the company that is owned by the ESOP is exempt from federal income taxes. For example, if your ESOP owns 80 percent of the company, you will only pay federal income tax on 20 percent of the shares.

> *King Arthur Flour has been one hundred percent employee owned since 1996. Through our employee stock ownership plan, the people who come to work here each day own a very real stake in the company and stand to benefit, or lose, based upon the company's success or failure. It's a real incentive to do our best work every day—to ensure that our products and service are always the best and our customers are happy.*

> Steve Voigt, CEO, King Arthur Flour
> BAKING GOODS—VERMONT

How Can You Implement This at Your Company?

If you want to explore this idea, talk to your employees to determine whether they are interested in or ready for such a plan. The following are some important questions for you and your employees to consider:

- Who should be eligible to participate in this plan?
- What is the minimum amount of time a worker should be employed before he or she starts earning ownership?
- Will employees have a say in company decision making? Do you think they will be ready for (or interested in) this type of participation?
- What internal systems will you need to implement to educate the new owners about their rights and responsibilities?
- How will your company manage the cultural difference between those who are employee owners and those who are not? How can your company build a culture of ownership and inclusion for the employees who do not wish to own stock or are not yet eligible?

If you have questions about employee ownership, I recommend reaching out to employee-owned B Corps such as Dansko, King Arthur Flour, Namaste Solar,

JUHUDI KILIMO

Nat Robinson, CEO, Juhudi Kilimo

ASSET-BASED FINANCING AND TRAINING—KENYA

Q: What business benefits do you directly attribute to your B Corp certification?

A: We decided to become a B Corporation because we wanted a way to distinguish our strong social mission from other companies in Kenya. This social mission is core to our business and is important for our clients, employees, partners, regulators, and other stakeholders to understand.

Because of our focus on serving rural, poor, smallholder farmers in Kenya, we are doing the work of many nongovernment organizations and social services organizations, but without any of the tax benefits or special treatment. The B Corp certification allowed us to receive some of the valuable benefits enjoyed by nonprofits, such as pro bono legal services and discounted software licenses.

Q: What was your biggest surprise about becoming a B Corp?

A: I was surprised at how many benefits we actually received as a B Corp in Kenya. We have received some fantastic discounts on the Salesforce licenses, which has dramatically changed the way we operate our business. This discount pushed us to migrate our entire IT [information technology] system to salesforce.com, and we are quickly becoming a microfinance leader in Kenya using this technology.

The mobile platform will dramatically improve the efficiency of our field officers in rural Kenya, since they will no longer need to carry paper books with them or visit a field office each day. This improved efficiency will drive better service to our clients, to help us move more rural smallholder farmers in Kenya out of poverty.

New Belgium Brewing Company, or Woodfold Manufacturing, among others. In addition, Praxis Consulting, a B Corp based in Philadelphia, is an expert in employee ownership and has assisted many businesses through this process.

For additional information on offering stock options, stock equivalents, and/or transferring ownership of the company to full-time employees, please see the Resources section in the back of the book.

✓ **Expand your company's health and wellness programs.**

Why Is This Rewarded?

This question rewards companies that promote healthy lifestyle choices for their employees. Typically, wellness programs focus on things like stress management, mental health, fitness, nutrition, and work–life balance.

In addition to benefiting individual workers, employee wellness programs have been shown to benefit a company's bottom line. For example, Johnson & Johnson estimates that its health and wellness program had a return on investment of $2.71 for every dollar spent between 2002 and 2008. A study of a different employer found an even higher return: every dollar invested in healthy interventions yielded $6 in health-care savings.[12]

One innovative way of reducing stress is to keep workers and their families closer together. Patagonia has provided subsidized, on-site child care since 1984. Founder Yvon Chouinard asserts that on-site child care is a profit center rather than a financial burden. "Seventy-one percent of our employees are women, and many occupy high-level management positions," says Chouinard. "Studies have shown that it costs a company an average of $50,000 to replace an employee—from recruiting costs, training, and loss of productivity. Our child-care center helps us retain our skilled moms."[13]

How Can You Implement This at Your Company?

There are many different things you can do to promote employee health and wellness. For example, B Corps offer a variety of benefits to workers, such as gardening classes, office yoga, discounted gym memberships, lunchtime running groups, organic fruit and healthy snacks, juicing classes, free access to a nutritionist, wellness goal-setting, or a company-hosted community supported agriculture program.

If you are inspired to create (or improve) your health and wellness program, consider talking to your insurance carrier about possible discounts and incentives. It is in their best interest to offer wellness options. The healthier your employees are, the fewer claims insurers will need to pay. In addition, try putting your health and wellness policy in writing. A formal policy is a useful communication tool that can help support a culture of wellness.

John Mackey of Whole Foods Market has an interesting approach to deciding which benefits to implement:

> *Every three years, we open up all the benefits for a mass vote. The leadership decides what percentage of the total revenue will go toward benefits for the company, and then assigns a cost for every potential benefit. Team members prioritize and vote on the benefits that they most prefer. This process results in benefits that reflect the needs and desires of the majority of the team members in the company. Team members often select benefits that the leadership did not necessarily think were good decisions. For example, they got rid of a benefit that paid people for community service hours, opting instead for more paid time off.[14]*

For additional information on expanding your company's health and wellness programs, please see the Resources section in the back of the book.

✓ **Create and distribute an employee handbook.**

Why Is This Rewarded?

An employee handbook is an important tool for communication between you and your employees. This handbook, when well written, explains your company's values, your expectations for your employees, your legal obligations as an employer, and your employees' rights, and describes what employees can expect from your company.

Having work rules and policies, however, means very little unless employees understand them. As a result, the assessment specifically rewards both creating the handbook and educating your employees about its contents.

How Can You Implement This at Your Company?

Employee handbooks typically cover the following topics:

- Company overview and philosophy
- Equal opportunity statement
- Work hours
- Pay schedules
- Performance review schedule and promotion process
- Benefits and time off
- Pension or profit-sharing plans
- Code of conduct
- Termination and grievance procedures

If your company does not have an employee handbook, see the Resources section in the back of the book for a template to help you get started. If you already have an employee handbook, evaluate how well you are communicating your policies and procedures. For example, many companies hold staff meetings on a semiannual or annual basis to discuss things such as changes in the company health-care plan or updates on the company's diversity and inclusion efforts.

✓ **Conduct regular, anonymous worker satisfaction and engagement surveys. Regularly collect (and make transparent) data on employee metrics such as retention, turnover, and diversity.**

Why Is This Rewarded?

How motivated and engaged are your employees? Over the past several years, research has identified a strong link between a company's financial performance and the engagement levels of its employees. For example, a recent Gallup study found that "organizations with engaged employees experience positive business performance, while workplaces with not engaged or actively disengaged employees are more likely to experience lower productivity."[15]

In addition, disengaged employees have been shown to have the same level of health problems as the unemployed, including higher rates of obesity and chronic illnesses. Gallup notes that "the high rates of obesity and chronic illnesses these groups report could have a major effect on their long-term health."[16] This research is especially troubling because 71 percent of American workers report that they are "not engaged" or are "actively disengaged" in their jobs.[17] Companies that regularly track metrics such as job satisfaction, retention, turnover, and diversity will have a better chance of identifying problems before they expand.

How Can You Implement This at Your Company?

Check to see if your local business journal or newspaper is conducting a Best Places to Work contest. These competitions usually require a company to conduct a thorough employee satisfaction or engagement survey. Sometimes the business journal or newspaper will also provide a local expert to help your company complete the survey. This can help you measure employee satisfaction and possibly win accolades from the press.

If you want to create your own employee engagement survey, Coro Strandberg suggests a few yes or no questions that you can ask your employees to better understand their level of knowledge and engagement:

- I am aware of and understand the [company's] strategy/policy and its core components.
- I believe my organization is making progress toward the implementation of the strategy/policy.
- The strategy/policy makes me feel good to be working for the organization.
- I believe the organization acts in alignment with [my personal values].
- I feel comfortable [expressing my concerns] in the workplace.
- I believe my organization is a champion of sustainability.[18]

The Honest Company has an internal website where employees can enter any sort of feedback (advice, suggestions, complaints, etc.) that goes directly to our head of [human resources]. These submissions are completely anonymous, unless someone chooses to include their info, and are taken very seriously.

Ashley King, Director of Social Goodness, The Honest Company
BABY ESSENTIALS, HEALTH AND WELLNESS PRODUCTS—CALIFORNIA

For additional information on worker satisfaction and engagement surveys and employee metrics, please see the Resources section in the back of the book.

✓ **Give employees part-time, flextime, or telecommuting options, as appropriate.**

Why Is This Rewarded?

Many businesses report that the recruitment and retention of skilled workers is one of the most important challenges they face. Workplace flexibility—giving people more control over their work time and schedules—has been shown to improve employee engagement, increase job satisfaction, and reduce stress. Workplace flexibility is also better for the bottom line. PricewaterhouseCoopers, for example, reported that implementing a flexible workplace program reduced its turnover rate by 24 percent.[19]

> *Renewable Choice Energy provides a wide variety of flexible work options for its employees, 90 percent of whom work at least partially from home. These options include part-time schedules, flextime, and telecommuting, to reduce travel emissions from employee commuting, increase productivity, and retain working parents. These benefits are extended to all positions, including those that are client-facing and administrative.*

Amy Haddon, Director of Business Operations, Renewable Choice Energy
CARBON OFFSETS AND SUSTAINABILITY CONSULTING—COLORADO

How Can You Implement This at Your Company?

A successful flexible work program requires clear organizational policies and guidelines. It requires managers to be knowledgeable about policies and to promote flexibility, to get the work done. It also requires employees to consider the needs of the job, their coworkers, customers, and the company when proposing flexible work strategies.

The following are some things to examine when considering a workplace flexibility program:

- What problem are you trying to address by increasing flexibility?
- What is your company's past experience with workplace flexibility?
- What tools and resources will you provide for your employees?
- How will you help your supervisors learn to manage employees who work flexibly?

- How will you communicate your new flexibility policy and procedures?
- How often will you review your program?

For additional information on providing employees with part-time, flextime, or telecommuting options, please see the Resources section in the back of the book.

✓ **Create an employee committee to monitor and advise on occupational health and safety.**

Why Is This Rewarded?

Although many industries have required safety regulations, this question recognizes employers who go above and beyond minimum industry standards.

Example: TS Designs

TS Designs, a B Corp–certified T-shirt printer based in North Carolina, created an innovative approach to worker health and safety. For example, most T-shirt printers use large vats of dye and steam, chemical fixing agents, and large drying units that can pose serious risks to their employees. TS Designs went above and beyond the basics by creating an employee-led safety committee and training series. The advantage of having this training led by employees rather than external experts is that the training tends to be far more relevant and useful, making it more likely that the safety information will be retained. In recent years, TS Designs also has identified a more powerful solution: using water-based inks that avoid certain hazardous processes in the first place.

How Can You Implement This at Your Company?

Create a safety committee that is led by employees and empowered to make changes. Suggestions from this committee will have greater credibility among other employees because the recommendations are coming from their peers. Moreover, because the people on the factory floor are more familiar with potential safety hazards, the committee's recommendations are often better than suggestions from management.

Another example is to convene a meeting with the company's product designers, sourcing experts, and/or process engineers. Because these individuals sit upstream of the manufacturing process, they can help you think of ways to avoid hazardous materials, processes, and by-products in the first place.

For additional information on monitoring and advising on occupational health and safety, please see the Resources section in the back of the book.

Reflections and Next Steps

Now that you have finished, take a moment to review the previous section, including any answers you gave on the Quick Assessment at the very beginning. Next, take a few minutes to write down your thoughts about the following questions. This will serve as a useful starting point for determining how you will move forward on your journey.

Based on the previous section, what resonates with me/my company?

What changes could we make that would have the greatest positive impact?

What are one or two easy wins?

What are one or two long-term goals?

Moving forward, who are the key players, potential allies, and coleaders?

Good for the Community

Why this matters: Job creation, diversity, civic engagement, and strong supply chains benefit your community and are sources of competitive advantage.

Civic Engagement and Giving

Local Involvement

Diversity

Suppliers, Distributors, and Product

Job Creation

Quick Assessment of Community Impact

Want to get a quick idea of how good your company is for the community? Take the following fifteen-item Quick Assessment to measure your performance over the past year. You can add up your total at the bottom for a rough idea of how you might score on this section of the B Impact Assessment.

Check the box if you and/or your company . . .

Job Creation

☐ create job opportunities for chronically underemployed populations, such as at-risk youth, homeless individuals, or individuals who were formerly incarcerated.

Diversity

☐ have a diverse board of directors, including women and minorities as well as disabled, low-income, or other previously excluded populations.

☐ have a diverse management team and employee base.

☐ have suppliers that are majority owned by women or individuals from under-represented populations.

Civic Engagement and Giving

☐ offer incentives for employees to organize service days and/or volunteer activities.

☐ set a goal to increase the percentage of employees who participate in service and/or volunteer activities.

☐ have a written community service policy.

☐ have a formal partnership to support a local charity.

☐ match charitable contributions made by employees.

☐ are a member of a third-party organization that certifies charitable giving, such as 1% for the Planet.

Local Involvement

☐ purchase goods and services from local, minority-owned, or woman-owned businesses.

☐ consider fair trade or environmental standards when making procurement decisions.

☐ bank with a local independent bank or credit union.

☐ bank with a Certified B Corporation, a community development financial institution, or a member of the Global Alliance for Banking on Values.

Suppliers, Distributors, and Product

☐ publicly disclose the social and environmental performance of your suppliers.

_____ Total

If you scored from **zero to 3**, you will have some work do to earn B Corp certification. Alternatively, you can make up ground with an outstanding performance in the other areas.

If you scored from **4 to 6**, you are a good candidate for B Corp certification, assuming you perform similarly well on the other sections.

If you scored from **7 to 15**, fantastic work! You are likely well on your way to getting the score you need for B Corp certification.

To see how your company stacks up against thousands of other businesses and for more best practice guides and resources, go to **www.bimpactassessment.net**. Don't worry; it's free and confidential.

T he first step to being good for the community is to see your business as connected to the local, national, and global communities in which it resides. Indeed, businesses that behave like socially and environmentally responsible citizens can benefit from an improved ability to attract and retain top talent, to generate positive media attention, and to increase customer goodwill.

The B Impact Assessment measures your company's community impact in five areas: job creation, which includes hiring locally and creating jobs for chronically underemployed populations; diversity, which includes having a diverse board of directors, management team, employee base, and supply chain; civic engagement and giving, which looks at employee volunteerism and charitable donations; local involvement, such as banking with an independent, local financial institution and supporting local, minority-owned, or women-owned businesses; and suppliers, distributors, and product, which includes such things as increasing transparency by publicly disclosing the social and environmental performance of your supply chain.

As in the Good for Workers section, I will highlight some of these topics, discuss why they are important, explain why they are rewarded on the assessment, and offer you tips for implementing these practices in your company.

✓ **Create job opportunities for chronically underemployed populations, such as at-risk youth, homeless individuals, or individuals who were formerly incarcerated.**

Why Is This Practice Rewarded?

Individuals with a history of incarceration, homelessness, or drug use face many barriers to employment, which may include insufficient job skills, a lack of access to transportation, or disabling health conditions. Individuals who successfully obtain a job may find it difficult to stay employed without access to a wide variety of supportive services. Many veterans, refugees, and people with disabilities face similar barriers.

Several innovative B Corporations, such as Cascade Engineering, Greyston Bakery, and Rubicon Bakery, provide chronically underemployed individuals with the employment, skills, and resources to lift themselves out of poverty. Some specific innovative B Corp programs include the following:

- DePaul Industries in Portland, Oregon, trains people with physical and mental disabilities for high-quality jobs in food manufacturing, co-packing, or security services. Over the past five years, DePaul has employed more than five thousand people and paid more than $43 million in wages.

- Susty Party in Brooklyn, New York, which makes eco-friendly party supplies, partnered with the Clovernook Center for the Blind and Visually Impaired to manufacture Susty Party's certified compostable, nontoxic, sustainably sourced paper cups.

- Britec in Santiago, Chile, trains inmates in Chilean prisons to manufacture solar hot water heaters. The trainees benefit from engineering skills that are transferrable to the job market and a reserve of cash that they can use after they are released from prison.

Example: Greyston Bakery

Greyston Bakery, a Certified B Corporation that is best known for baking the brownies in Ben & Jerry's Chocolate Fudge Brownie ice cream, is located in the impoverished community of Southwest Yonkers, New York.

Greyston's open hiring policy offers employment opportunities to anyone, regardless of educational attainment, work history, or previous incarceration, homelessness, or drug use. Anyone that comes to the front door of the bakery is given the chance to work, no questions asked. Greyston provides its workers with resources, personal development tools, and professional training, to give them the greatest chance of success in their new position.

GoLite®
Kim Coupounas,
Cofounder, GoLite
OUTDOOR APPAREL—COLORADO

Q: What business benefits do you directly attribute to your B Corp certification?

A: The benefits we have received include:

- increased employee and customer engagement, understanding of our sustainability work, and loyalty to the company and brand.
- improved operations, performance, and reporting on the full set of sustainability dimensions. By simply asking the questions on certain dimensions and showing best practices, the B Corp certification process prompted us to make changes in our business operations.
- a living, breathing network of like-minded people and business connections.
- increased sales from both mainstream and conscious consumers.

Q: What was the biggest challenge you had to overcome to certify as a B Corp?

A: Aside from me, our executive team was unfamiliar with the B Corporation certification in 2008, when we originally certified. They didn't know B Lab and they had to be persuaded to invest the staff time and money into certifying. Now it is a no-brainer for us and there is zero hesitation from anyone in management in committing the resources necessary to recertify.

Q: What was your biggest surprise about becoming a B Corp?

A: How much the affiliation value mattered to us, internally. We always knew we were working hard and were proud of our work, but we didn't have a reference point for people to be able to say *how* good we were relative to other companies. To be able to say that we are in the same company as Seventh Generation, Method, New Belgium, Ben & Jerry's, et al. is a *very* big deal. It takes a young and—in many geographic areas—unknown brand and gives us automatic credibility as a legitimate player.

Example: Cascade Engineering

Cascade Engineering's Welfare to Career program aims to help people find fulfilling and long-term employment. Cascade's program, which has an average retention rate of 97 percent, is based on two key principles: partnering with the State of Michigan to offer on-site support to Welfare to Career participants, and educating key company leaders about the principles contained in the book *A Framework for Understanding Poverty.*[a]

The success of the Welfare to Career program has benefitted individual workers, the local community, and Cascade Engineering's bottom line. A Stanford Business School case study estimates that Cascade's savings over a five-year period totaled $502,000, a result of lower contracting costs, wage subsidies, and tax credits.[b] The program also provides $900,000 in savings to the State of Michigan, which has to pay less into welfare programs and sees increased tax receipts.

a. Ruby K. Payne, *A Framework for Understanding Poverty* (Highlands, TX: aha! Process, 1996).

b. James Bradley, "Bridging the Cultures of Business & Poverty: Welfare to Career at Cascade Engineering," *Stanford Social Innovation Review,* http://www.cascadeng.com/sites/default/files/bridging-cultures-stansford-cs.pdf.

How Can You Implement This at Your Company?

Although innovative employment programs take time to build, there are some basic steps that you and your team can take to determine whether a similar partnership is possible for your company.

Many communities already have organizations that work with disabled, homeless, or formerly incarcerated individuals. Reach out to these organizations to see whether they work with local businesses to create employment opportunities for their clients. If there is mutual interest, try offering to help on a short project and/or organizing an employee volunteer day at their facility. This is a great way to help determine whether you and your company are passionate about the organization's cause and whether a more formal partnership would be a good fit.

Many organizations that work with chronically underemployed populations will also help you design, modify, and implement a training program to meet specific needs. For example, Evergreen Lodge, a Certified B Corporation based in California's Yosemite National Park, works with a nonprofit called Juma Ventures to design and implement a summer training program for at-risk youth. Evergreen Lodge's program provides career-oriented training and work experience, includes intensive social services support, and exposes participants to a rich set of outdoor and recreational life experiences.

For additional information on creating job opportunities for chronically underemployed populations, please see the Resources section in the back of the book.

✓ **Expand the diversity of your board of directors, management team, and suppliers so that they represent a range of cultures, religious beliefs, ethnicities, sexual orientations, physical abilities, and genders.**

Why Is This Practice Rewarded?

The benefits of diversity, particularly gender diversity, are well documented. For example, McKinsey found that companies with a high representation of female executives have a 47 percent higher average return on equity than other businesses.[20] Likewise, Credit Suisse found that companies with one or more female board members have superior share price performance relative to industry peers with all-male boards of directors.[21]

More studies are starting to show that these benefits also apply when working with other diverse groups, such as ethnic minorities, people with disabilities, and lesbian, gay, bisexual, and transgender communities. For example, one study found that employees of gay managers tend to have 35 percent higher job satisfaction and engagement.[22]

Despite the wide diversity of religious beliefs, ethnicities, sexual orientations, physical abilities, and genders in society, most of these communities are vastly underrepresented at the senior executive level. For example, women represent approximately 50 percent of the workforce but represent only 17 percent of board seats of companies in the Fortune 1000.[23] However, thanks to the efforts of many forward-thinking businesses, advocates, and industry associations, diversity at all management levels is starting to rise.

Example: Home Care Associates

A great example of diversity from the B Corp community is Home Care Associates, a company that provides in-home care to clients in the Philadelphia area. Home Care Associates is 95 percent owned by women, is led by women, and specifically targets for hiring and promotion women from ethnic minority and/or low-income communities

How Can You Implement This at Your Company?

Expanding the diversity of your company is incredibly worthwhile. The following are a few tips to help you on your journey:

- When hiring, intentionally reach out to communities that are unlikely to have heard about your company. For example, create a relationship with schools in your area that have a diverse student body. Talk to community organizations to help find candidates.

- Engage your current employees to get feedback, ideas, and referrals. Ask an employee to be in charge of finding ways to incorporate or celebrate the cultural differences within the company.

- Reach out to a local B Corp and ask them about their experiences with creating a diverse leadership team and/or workforce.

- For additional information on increasing the diversity of your board, management, and suppliers, please see the Resources section in the back of the book.

✓ **Offer incentives for employees to organize service days and/or volunteer activities, and set a goal to increase the percentage of employees who participate. Communicate your efforts through a written community service policy.**

Why Is This Practice Rewarded?

Volunteers provide a tremendous amount of support to nonprofit organizations around the globe. In the United States, for example, roughly 61 million people volunteer annually, at a value of $162 billion.[24]

—COOK—

Edward Perry, Cofounder and Managing Director, COOK Trading

FROZEN READY MEALS—UNITED KINGDOM

Q: Why did you become a B Corp?

A: From the founding of COOK in 1997, the ambition for the business was about more than money, and having a positive social impact. Translating this desire into something tangible that our management team could build a plan around was proving difficult. It was so countercultural. Becoming a B Corporation—which we see as one hundred percent aligned with our principles—has given us a context and reference point for what we were trying to achieve all along.

We feel that B Corp is a "No Bullshit" stamp that proves we mean what we say and is a great way to start a conversation about how and why our business is different.

Q: What surprised you from your experience at the B Corp Champions Retreat?

A: Being in the United Kingdom, we hadn't met any other B Corps before the Champions Retreat in Boulder. We were pretty confident we agreed with what the B Corp movement stood for, but we didn't know if we'd really fit into the community. Well, the four senior team members who attended enjoyed two of the best days of their working lives. The sense of shared purpose was overwhelming.

The Champions Retreat wasn't a talking shop of politicians or well-meaning academics and community leaders; these were the people who were running successful and innovative businesses on the front line. The B Corp community was absolutely aligned by this common goal and totally committed to furthering its cause. It was inspiring, affirming, extremely exhausting, and enormous fun.

This question rewards companies that measure, compare, and increase the percentage of employees who volunteer in the local community. Companies typically provide incentives such as paid time off, company-organized service days, or other perks (such as preferred parking spots) to increase participation.

> We allow our employees to take up to twenty hours a year to volunteer for a nonprofit of their choice. Not only do we give employees the time off, we pay them their salary while they do, and make a matching donation to the organization that they are volunteering for. So now, not only are we shipping shoes, but we're shipping shoes to help support the nonprofits our team is invested in. This furthers their engagement both in the community and in Dansko. It's a win-win from our standpoint.

Marc Vettori, Director of Human Resources, Dansko
FOOTWEAR—PENNSYLVANIA

Creating service and volunteer opportunities for your employees is good for business. The Center for Corporate Citizenship at Boston College, for example, reports that employee volunteer programs enhance employee attraction, recruitment, loyalty, and skills as well as a company's image in the community.[25] In addition, according to the study *Good Companies, Better Employees*, employee volunteer programs increase positive word of mouth from employees about their employers, improve worker satisfaction, and increase employee retention rates.[26]

How Can You Implement This at Your Company?

There are many different approaches to encouraging community service at your workplace. The first step is to have a conversation with your employees. The following are some examples of questions to discuss:

- Which community service opportunities are employees most interested in?
- Are there opportunities that enable employees to utilize their professional skills?
- How will your volunteer program contribute to business goals?
- Who will be responsible for volunteer coordination?
- Who will be responsible for creating a written community service policy and tracking the number of participating employees?

- Will you offer incentives to participate?
- How can you make the culture of volunteering more fun?

By engaging your workers in the initial discussions, brainstorming, and creation of the program, you will have a much better chance of strong employee participation.

We have something at Ben & Jerry's called the Joy Gang. The Joy Gang is a volunteer team of employees that come up with random activities—generally about once a month, but sometimes more, if so moved—to make work life a bit more fun. This includes celebrating traditional and oddball holidays with appropriate cultural food and info sharing, such as Dyngus Day (Polish Easter Monday), Tie-Day Fridays (which involves dressing up, since we are a T-shirt and jeans culture), and the Dog Days of Summer (free dog washes for employee dogs).

Rob Michalak, Global Director of Social Mission, Ben & Jerry's
ICE CREAM—VERMONT

The following are some ideas to help encourage your employees to volunteer:

- Inform employees about volunteer opportunities through bulletin board notices, pay packet inserts, newsletters, intranet, links to volunteer databases, and/or volunteer fairs.
- Offer paid time off specifically to pursue volunteer opportunities.
- Assign a volunteer coordinator to develop and oversee volunteer activities.
- Match individuals who possess particular management and technical skills with nonprofit agencies that request help in those areas of expertise.
- Encourage a culture of volunteerism by giving awards to employees for community service.
- Encourage employees to volunteer to sit on a board of directors at a local nonprofit.

In addition, I recommend reaching out to B Corps such as Catchafire, Micro-Edge, and NobleHour that have expertise in connecting employees to volunteer activities and designing effective volunteer programs.

For additional information on creating a community service policy, please see the Resources section in the back of the book.

✓ **Formalize your charitable giving program. Consider creating a partnership with a local charity, matching charitable contributions made by your employees, and joining a third-party organization that certifies charitable giving, such as 1% for the Planet.**

Why Is This Practice Rewarded?

If you and your employees prefer to work with a specific charity, consider creating a formal partnership with that organization. These types of formal partnerships are important because many nonprofits struggle with a lack of consistent donations. This lack of consistency can force nonprofits to focus on short-term funding issues rather than concentrating on furthering their mission.

For those who are interested in donating money, I highly recommend looking at 1% for the Planet. Members of 1% for the Planet pledge to donate at least 1 percent of their annual sales to an extensive list of environmental nonprofits. In addition, by joining 1% for the Planet and designating B Lab as your donation recipient, you can offset your B Corp certification fees.[27]

A charity partnership, however, does not have to be limited to financial donations. Your company could donate employee time, free products, or services or allow the charity to use your facilities for trainings or events.

Example: Luscious Garage

Luscious Garage, a B Corp auto repair shop that specializes in hybrids, donates its shop space for the monthly meeting of the Golden Gate Electric Vehicle Association. The GGEVA is a high-tech group of transportation activists who work with vehicle manufacturers, government agencies, nonprofits, and individuals to promote electric vehicles and the expansion of an electric charging infrastructure.

How Can You Implement This at Your Company?

If your company is interested in making financial contributions, I suggest organizing a meeting with your team to discuss creating a written charitable giving policy and a line item in your budget for donations. Even if you have already passed the budgeting process for this year, I recommend having this conversation for next year's budget.

Another good idea is to ask your employees or customers where they are donating already. Choosing a cause that your stakeholders already care about will get everyone excited and lead to better participation in your campaign.

Example: Etsy

Etsy's core competency is its team of talented software developers and engineers. Etsy recognizes that there is a growing need for more talented programmers, particularly women, to meet the demands of the future. As a result, Etsy supports the Hacker School, a three-month, full-time program in New York that teaches people how to become better programmers. In 2012 Etsy provided ten Hacker Grants of $5,000 each—a total of $50,000—to women who wanted to join but needed financial support to do so. Etsy's goal is to encourage more women to join engineering at Etsy and across the industry.

Example: Give Something Back Office Supplies

Give Something Back Office Supplies donates the majority of its profits to local charities every year. To identify which charities to support, Give Something Back asks its customers, community members, and employees to vote in an annual ballot. Over the past twenty-three years, Give Something Back has donated more than $5 million to nonprofits in the local communities that it serves.

For additional information on formalizing your charitable giving program, please see the Resources section in the back of the book.

✓ **Purchase goods and services from local, minority-owned, or woman-owned businesses. Consider fair trade or environmental standards when making procurement decisions.**

Why Is This Practice Rewarded?

This question rewards businesses that purchase from companies owned by women, ethnic minorities, veterans, or ex-offenders, or from companies located in low-income communities. These procurement practices can benefit a wide variety of stakeholders. For example, purchasing local goods and services will help support job creation within your community, will keep tax dollars invested in community projects, and will reduce the environmental impact of long-distance shipping. This question also rewards companies that purchase materials, ingredients, or services that have been certified to meet minimum social and/or environmental standards.

Example: Preserve

Preserve purchases 100 percent recycled plastic to use in its cups, bowls, toothbrushes, and other products. This helps reduce the chemical-, energy-, and water-intensive steps of extracting and refining virgin plastic and helps create a more viable market by stimulating demand for postconsumer recycled materials.

How Can You Implement This at Your Company?

First, learn more about your suppliers and the products you purchase from them. Some of this information can be gleaned from your supplier's website or from product packaging. For more detailed information, however, you will probably have to contact your supplier directly.

Another valuable step is to encourage your suppliers to benchmark their social and environmental performance via the free B Impact Assessment. This will give you a comprehensive snapshot of the overall performance of your supply chain and will give your suppliers a variety of tools, resources, and best practices to help them focus on continual improvement.

Tom Payne, Marketing Director, King Arthur Flour

BAKING GOODS—VERMONT

Q: What business benefits do you directly attribute to your B Corp certification?

A: We have received a number of benefits, including:

- King Arthur Flour has been mentioned in sixty-four articles between 2008 and the present (including print, online publications, and blogs), reaching over 72 million readers. Highlights include pieces in *Fast Company*, the *Christian Science Monitor*, Care2, the *San Francisco Chronicle*, and the *Denver Post*.

- We have received about $50,000 in free print ads through the B Corp brand campaign. We have also saved $46,000 on twenty Salesforce licenses through B Lab's partnership with the Salesforce Foundation.

Q: What was your biggest surprise about becoming a B Corp?

A: It surprises me that every company doesn't jump on board immediately. The accountability keeps us on track with our stewardship goals and allows us to have a corporate structure that includes the triple bottom line. The transparency also gives our customers, employees, and board a clear understanding of how we are doing good and gives them confidence that we are walking the walk in addition to talking the talk. It also helps us pinpoint where we still have room for growth.

Q: What advice do you have for a business that is considering B Corp certification?

A: Do it. While you may find the process of evaluating your business a bit time consuming, and perhaps—though hopefully not—disheartening, the process and the designation can only make your company better.

For additional information on creating a purchasing policy, please see the Resources section in the back of the book.

✓ **Bank with a local independent bank or credit union. Choose a bank that is a Certified B Corporation, a community development financial institution, or a member of the Global Alliance for Banking on Values.**

Why Is This Practice Rewarded?

Voting with your dollars extends beyond responsible purchasing decisions. It is also important to think about where you keep your money—and how your money is being invested. Vince Siciliano, president and CEO of New Resource Bank, says, "One question we like to ask is 'Where does your money spend the night?' Most people don't realize that when they deposit their money in a bank account, it's being invested. So, do they invest their money with an institution that uses it for projects that they would be ashamed to be associated with, or do they invest it with an institution that will invest it in ways that support their values? We believe that banking can be more than just a service—it can be a way to create a better world."

Many locally owned banks and credit unions offer the same array of services as big banks, from online bill paying to debit and credit cards, at a lower cost. In addition, loan approvals and other decisions are made by people who live in the community, have face-to-face relationships with their customers, and understand local needs. Because of this personal knowledge, local financial institutions are often able to approve loans that big banks would reject.

How Can You Implement This at Your Company?

If you are considering switching, there are a number of questions to ask prospective financial institutions, including the following:

- Do you have any socially or environmentally responsible banking practices?
- Are there any industries in which you specialize?
- Are there any industries that you avoid?
- What size company do you most often finance and serve?
- Do you participate in the Small Business Association loan program?

For additional information on selecting a local independent bank or credit union, please see the Resources section in the back of the book.

✓ **Publicly disclose the social and environmental performance of your suppliers.**

Why Is This Practice Rewarded?

This question rewards businesses that promote safe working conditions, treat workers with respect and dignity, and/or use environmentally responsible manufacturing processes. Supply chain transparency is especially important if your company sources a majority of its products from developing countries, where enforcement of environmental and labor laws can vary widely.

In addition, consumers are increasingly curious about where and how their products are made. A recent report by Cohn & Wolfe states, "Transparency has become more important in the past year, and now stands alongside quality and price in the decision-making process for consumers." Supply chain transparency is particularly important for businesses, given the rise of social media and the availability of information. Cohn & Wolfe found that "half of consumers would stop buying a product or a service if they found out the company did not reflect their personal values, whilst 30 percent would encourage their friends and families to do the same. A quarter would go even further and support a boycott of the company."[28]

Improved supply chain transparency also has been shown to benefit shareholders. In a study conducted by the University of California, Davis, and the University of California, Berkeley, researchers tracked the stock prices of companies that voluntarily disclosed their carbon emissions data and reduction targets. The study found that in the days after this information was disclosed, the companies saw their stock prices increase significantly. The stock prices of smaller companies performed particularly well, with average increases of 2.32 percent.[29]

In a similar study, the Carbon Disclosure Project found that companies that are leaders in addressing climate change "tend to perform better, not only in terms of greenhouse gas emissions management but also in terms of financial performance," providing approximately twice the average return on investment as the Global 500 from January 2005 to May 2011.[30]

How Can You Implement This at Your Company?

The first step toward improving supply chain transparency is to get a baseline of your supply chain's overall social and environmental performance. In my opinion, the best (free) means of benchmarking this performance is to ask your suppliers to take the B Impact Assessment.[31]

Set goals to increase your supply chain transparency over time. Increased transparency can help you generate consumer trust, improve your brand value, and build thought leadership in your industry. In addition, try to encourage and assist your suppliers in pursuing third-party certification. This can benefit your company by increasing independent, verified accountability within its supply chain and can benefit your supplier by helping it to attract more mission-aligned customers.

Reflections and Next Steps

Now that you have finished, take a moment to review the previous section, including any answers you gave on the Quick Assessment at the very beginning. Next, take a few minutes to write down your thoughts about the following questions. This will serve as a useful starting point for determining how you will move forward on your journey.

Based on the previous section, what resonates with me/my company?

What changes could we make that would have the greatest positive impact?

What are one or two easy wins?

What are one or two long-term goals?

Moving forward, who are the key players, potential allies, and coleaders?

Good for the Environment

Why this matters: Sustainability is a source of innovation. Improving your environmental performance can help you attract top talent, create more durable relationships with suppliers, and increase consumer trust.

Transportation, Distribution, and Suppliers

Energy, Water, and Materials

Emissions and Waste

Land, Office and Plant

Quick Assessment of Environmental Impact

Want to get an idea of how good your company is for the environment? Take the following fourteen-item Quick Assessment to measure your performance over the past year. You can add up your total at the bottom for a rough idea of how you might score on the Environment section of the B Impact Assessment.

Check the box if you and/or your company . . .

Land, Office, and Plant

☐ conduct an annual environmental audit of your energy, water, and waste efficiency.

☐ make the results of the environmental audit transparent to the public.

☐ use energy-efficient lighting systems (e.g., natural light, LEDs, CFLs, occupancy sensors, daylight dimmers, or task lighting).

☐ use energy-efficient office equipment (e.g., Energy Star appliances, automatic sleep modes, or after-hours timers).

☐ use energy-efficient heating and air-conditioning systems (e.g., programmable thermostats, timers, occupancy sensors, or double-paned windows).

☐ use water-efficient systems (e.g., low-flow toilets, faucets, or showerheads) or harvest rainwater.

☐ have solar panels, solar water heaters, or on-site wind, biomass, or other renewable energy systems.

☐ purchase renewable energy credits to offset any nonrenewable energy that you use.

☐ monitor and improve indoor air quality at your facilities.

☐ provide employees with incentives to use alternative commuting options to get to work.

With Gratitude

Huge thanks to author Ryan Honeyman and publisher Berrett-Koehler for creating this platform to highlight the inspiring work of so many and the leadership of the entire B Corp community in *The B Corp Handbook: How to Use Business as a Force For Good.*

Please use The B Corp Handbook as a tool to enhance your individual and organizational thought leadership, engage your team, and help us achieve our collective vision.

Additional copies are available to purchase at a 50% discount to share with your team, partners, and network.

Email Sarah Haggarty at shaggarty@bcorporation.net for details.

Let's Build the Movement Together

This fall, the B Corp community will host 100 events in 100 days to invite all companies to use business as a force for good.

Please find a partner organization to co-host a Build a Better Business workshop featuring you, other B Corps, and The Handbook. B Lab will provide 50 free copies for attendees of your event.

Email event details to thelab@bcorporation.net to get a full event toolkit with template agenda, invites, presentation, moderator guide.

Energy, Water, and Materials

☐ conduct life cycle assessments of your products.

Emissions and Waste

☐ monitor and record your greenhouse gas emissions.

☐ have a reclamation program to recycle or reuse end products.

Transport, Distribution, and Suppliers

☐ encourage suppliers to start their own environmental reviews or audits, which may cover energy, water, waste, carbon emissions, renewables, or materials.

_____ Total

If you scored from **zero to 3,** you will have some work do to earn B Corp certification. Alternatively, you can make up ground with an outstanding performance in the other areas.

If you scored from **4 to 6,** you are a good candidate for B Corp certification, assuming you perform similarly well on the other sections.

If you scored from **7 to 14,** fantastic work! You are likely well on your way to getting the score you need for B Corp certification.

To see how your company stacks up against thousands of other businesses and for more best practice guides and resources, go to **www.bimpactassessment.net.** Don't worry; it's free and confidential.

Being good for the environment is good for your company's bottom line. Many businesses, such as Ben & Jerry's, Method, and Patagonia, have found that improving their environmental performance has increased their profits by helping them attract top talent, create more durable relationships with suppliers, and increase consumer trust.

In the past few years, many Fortune 500 companies have made a dramatic strategic shift toward sustainability. For example, Walmart is committed to using 100 percent renewable energy, Coca-Cola is using plant-based bottles, and McDonald's is serving Fair Trade Certified coffee in many of its stores. As we have noted, McKinsey says, "The choice for companies today is not if, but *how* they should manage their sustainability activities."[32]

This section assesses your environmental impact in four areas: land, office, and plant, which includes increasing your energy, water, and waste efficiency, using renewable energy, encouraging employees to use alternative commuting options, and improving your building's indoor air quality; energy, water, and materials, which includes conducting a life cycle assessment of your products; emissions and waste, which includes starting a product reclamation program and monitoring your greenhouse gas emissions; and transport, distribution, and suppliers, which includes encouraging your suppliers to improve their environmental performance.

As in the previous sections, I will discuss why these topics are important and explain how you can implement these practices in your company.

✓ **Conduct an annual environmental audit of your energy, water, and waste efficiency and make the results transparent to the public.**

Why Is This Practice Rewarded?

An environmental audit is a tool that can help your company identify its environmental impact, determine whether it is meeting certain environmental performance criteria, and better understand how it can improve its performance in the future.

This question rewards companies that make the results of their environmental audit transparent to the public. This disclosure not only serves to inform and educate the public but also provides an incentive for your company to maintain its practices over time.

Environmental audits vary depending on the size of the business. A small business, for example, may concentrate primarily on paper, water, and energy use, whereas a large organization may also evaluate emissions, materials, hazardous waste, travel, commuting, and its corporate fleet.

How Can You Implement This at Your Company?

I recommend starting with energy efficiency, because it is relatively easy to implement and directly benefits your bottom line. Try benchmarking your building with the free Energy Star Portfolio Manager software.[33] Portfolio Manager compares your facility's energy performance to similar buildings across the United States. After you input your building's monthly energy data, Portfolio Manager gives your building a score from 1 to 100, with 50 being the national average. If your facility scores below 50, it is a red flag that you are wasting energy and money.

Although individual audit results will vary, the following are some of the most common opportunities to save money and reduce your environmental footprint:

Lighting and Equipment

- Use task lighting instead of lighting an entire area.
- Replace incandescent exit lighting with LEDs.
- Install lighting occupancy sensors.
- Make sure exterior lighting is turned off during the daytime.
- Clean lighting fixtures, diffusers, and lamps annually—dirt can reduce lighting efficiency by up to 50 percent.
- Program sleep modes for computers, copiers, and other equipment, to power them down when they are not in use, at night, and on weekends.

Heating and Air-Conditioning

- Install programmable thermostats.
- Replace or install new insulation in exterior walls, ceilings, and wall cavities.
- Install double-pane windows where appropriate.

tomorrow's agenda

Terence Jeyaretnam, Executive Director, Net Balance

SUSTAINABILITY CONSULTING—AUSTRALIA

Q: How did your company sell the idea of becoming a B Corp, internally?

A: For Net Balance, becoming a B Corporation was simply an extension of our vision and values. We believe that, for business to succeed into the future, it must be led by purpose as much as profit. B Corporation certification reflects our belief that the natural selection process will redefine business success in the new economy—what we call "tomorrow's agenda."

As one of the founding B Corporations in Australia, this is a great opportunity for us to share with our clients the importance of the certification and to help drive the movement in Australia and Asia–Pacific.

Q: What business benefits do you directly attribute to your B Corp certification?

A: The B Corp certification allows companies to show they have been reviewed by a third party, building trust as well as brand credibility for customers, shareholders, and employees. The B Corp community also encourages B Corporations to do business directly with other B Corporations, by offering particular exclusive benefits.

But at the heart of it, B Corp gives us a name—a catchcry—to explain what Net Balance is all about. For years we have been trying to explain that we're here for a purpose: to create social change and to get business and government ready for the challenges of tomorrow. The certification says that in one letter!

- Repaint the exterior of the building and the roof. Choose light colors that reflect sunlight.
- Build a roof garden.
- Install automatic blinds that open during winter daylight hours and close during summer daylight hours.

Water

- Install low-flow toilets, urinals, faucets, and shower heads.
- Check for toilet leaks by using leak-detecting tablets, which may be available from your water company.
- Irrigate landscapes with gray water from domestic activities such as laundry and bathing.
- Install a self-adjusting, weather-based irrigation controller that automatically tailors watering schedules to match local weather, plant types, and other site-specific conditions.
- When repaving parking lots, install permeable concrete or create berms to drain or direct water into plantings and to avoid storm water runoff.

For additional information on conducting an annual environmental audit of your energy, water, and waste efficiency, please see the Resources section in the back of the book.

✓ **Increase the amount of renewable energy you use annually.**

Why Is This on the Assessment?

Renewable energy includes electricity and heat generated from solar, wind, ocean, hydropower, biomass, geothermal, or hydrogen resources. You may already receive a percentage of renewable energy from your utility provider. In Northern California, for example, approximately 19 percent of electricity provided by the local utility is derived from renewable sources, which will earn you points on the B Impact Assessment.

How Can You Implement This at Your Company?

If you do not have an on-site source of renewable energy (e.g., solar panels, wind, or a geothermal system), or if your local utility provider does not have a green power program, you can purchase renewable energy credits to offset your carbon emissions.

> As a B Corporation it is important to be a leader and help demonstrate how renewable energy technology can address the hidden environmental and social costs of fossil fuels. At TS Designs we have two solar arrays, a micro wind turbine, a retail biodiesel station, and a biomass methane digester. Our investment in these technologies not only has helped the environment but also has been like a billboard to our customer base, showing that we walk the talk.

> Eric Henry, President, TS Designs
> CUSTOM T-SHIRTS—NORTH CAROLINA

For additional information on increasing your annual use of renewable energy, please see the Resources section in the back of the book.

✓ Monitor and improve indoor air quality at your facilities.

Why Is This on the Assessment?

Most people spend a large proportion of their day in buildings, homes, cars, and other manufactured structures. In the past several years, however, a growing body of research has shown that indoor air can be more polluted than outdoor air, even in the largest and most industrialized cities. Indoor air problems are often caused by ventilation system deficiencies, overcrowding, off-gassing from materials in offices and mechanical equipment, tobacco smoke, microbiological contamination, and outside air pollutants.

In addition, your company may have hazardous waste items that should not be thrown away with regular waste because they may pose a threat to human health or the environment. Examples include printer cartridges, batteries, and CFL bulbs.

How Can You Implement This at Your Company?

You can take the following steps to reduce the amount of harmful chemicals used by your company, improve indoor air quality at your offices, and dispose of waste responsibly:

- Get more plants. Common houseplants are natural air cleaners and can dramatically improve your indoor air quality. Spider plants, English ivy, and azaleas are great air cleaners.
- Require the use of nontoxic cleaning and janitorial products.
- Recycle universal wastes (e.g., spent fluorescent light tubes and bulbs, electronic equipment, and batteries) as required by law.[34]
- All products made from petroleum give off volatile organic compounds. These are chemical compounds that cause asthma and cancer. Purchase building products and materials that contain no or low levels of VOCs. For example, a room freshly painted with non-VOC paint won't give you nausea or headaches.
- Eliminate the routine use of all disinfectants and sanitizers, unless they are required for compliance with environmental health codes.
- Replace standard fluorescent lights with no-mercury LED lights.
- Use unbleached and/or chlorine-free paper products (e.g., copy paper, paper towels, napkins, or coffee filters).
- Print promotional materials with vegetable or other low-VOC inks.

For additional information on monitoring your building's indoor air quality, please see the Resources section in the back of the book.

✓ **Provide employees with incentives to use alternative commuting options to get to work.**

Why Is This Practice Rewarded?

Employers that encourage alternative commuting, such as carpooling, vanpooling, use of public transit, bicycling, or telework, have been shown to have happier workers, enhanced job performance, and higher employee retention rates.[35] Alternative commuting also promotes an environmentally friendly workplace and helps to keep traffic off the roads.

> *GoLite actively encourages alternative transportation to work for our employees through participation in Bike to Work Day, Week, and Month, a bike-friendly office, recognizing Commuter(s) of the Year with cash awards, and providing cash incentives for selecting more energy-efficient modes of*

Kenyatta Brame, Chief Administrative Officer, Cascade Engineering

MANUFACTURING—MICHIGAN

Q: What business benefits do you directly attribute to your B Corp certification?

A: One of the biggest benefits is collaboration. The certification gives us an opportunity to get to know B Lab and other B Corps, learn from them, and share with them our best practices. The certification also keeps us alert to improvement opportunities within the company and to the changing sustainable business climate outside the company.

Q: What was the biggest challenge you had to overcome to certify as a B Corp?

A: Cascade Engineering under Fred Keller's leadership has been a triple bottom line–focused company for over a decade now. Even with our existing practices, the certification process challenged us to look at a few areas we had not considered before. The entire process is very rigorous, which assures transparency and a well-documented commitment to the principles of B Corp certification.

Q: What was your biggest surprise about becoming a B Corp?

A: The biggest surprise for us is to see the increasing number of companies, both small and large, here in the U.S. and abroad, that are joining the movement every day. When we first became a Certified B Corp in 2010 there were only about three hundred other certified companies, almost all in the United States, and we were the largest of them all. The situation is very different today, and we are no longer the largest Certified B Corp. Now there are thousands of B Corps in thirty-plus countries.

travel. For every ten times a person bikes, walks, or runs to and from the office from home, we give them $10 for a "free" lunch. Other alternative means of transportation, such as public transport, ride share, motorcycle, and hybrid vehicle, are given partial credit.

Kim Coupounas, Cofounder, GoLite
OUTDOOR APPAREL—COLORADO

How Can You Implement This at Your Company?

Engage your employees in a discussion about alternative commuting. The key is to keep trying new ideas, to solicit feedback, and to continue to adjust as needed. The following few questions may help start the conversation:

- Will subsidies or financial incentives for alternative commuting be provided?
- Will nonfinancial incentives such as prizes and awards be offered?
- Is there a need to construct new facilities, such as showers for bicyclists?
- Can the company work with existing regional transit services, such as ride matching or the Guaranteed Ride Home program, or is there a need to co-ordinate those internally?
- How much staff time will be required to administer the program?
- Are employment levels at your company expected to change in the next few years? The answer to this question may help you plan your initiative to better meet future trends.
- Are there clusters of employees with common commute characteristics (e.g., home location and arrival/departure times)? This information can be helpful for employees who are looking for ride-share matches.
- Which alternative commuting options are employees most willing to try? Survey your employees to find out.

✓ **Conduct a life cycle assessment of your products.**

Why Is This Practice Rewarded?

A life cycle assessment helps a company see the complete picture of its products' environmental impact. For a typical product, LCAs take into account the harvesting of raw materials, transport, manufacturing, product packaging, the use of the product, and disposal of the product and packaging after use. LCAs have been done on a variety of products, including jet engines, diapers, drinking cups, and computers.

There are many reasons for your company to conduct a life cycle assessment. It can be used to reduce your environmental footprint, eliminate waste, reduce costs, support marketing claims, or improve your brand's image. An LCA also creates common metrics that can be compared and shared with your employees, suppliers, and partners.

LCAs often reveal surprising—and useful—discoveries. For example, Walmart conducted an LCA and found that fertilizer is responsible for half of the carbon footprint in its supply chain. Walmart is now working with its suppliers to reduce the amount of fertilizer it uses. Because of Walmart's size, this has the potential to reduce the carbon footprint of more than 30 percent of food and beverage sales in North America.

In the biofuels business, a life cycle analysis (LCA) is critically important. While calculating an LCA is scientific and complex, a simple way of thinking about it is to answer the question, "How many fossil units of energy go into the creation of a gallon of fuel, versus how many renewable units of energy are returned?" One reason this is important is because if the return is not high enough, perhaps the fuel should not be made at all. We had a vague sense of this at Piedmont Biofuels.

Then we became a B Corporation. In taking the assessment, we realized that our early work in LCA was important not only to our industry but also to every industry on earth. We hired an independent consulting firm to analyze our data and create a standard methodology, and we published that on the web. At one point, we decided to host an LCA Night at our plant, where we could discuss the topic with our customers, employees, members, and stakeholders. We set out twelve chairs for the event, thinking it might attract a few energy nerds outside of ourselves. Thirty-five people showed up, and a rousing discussion ensued.

Now we do an annual formal LCA on our fuel, and our employees treat it like a scorecard. We use our LCA not only for our B Corp recertification but also have relied upon it for our certification with the Roundtable on Sustainable Biomaterials. Thanks to B Corp, our LCA is now an important part of our culture and something we have become known for.

Lyle Estill, Founder, Piedmont Biofuels
BIOFUELS—NORTH CAROLINA

How Can You Implement This at Your Company?

Completing a life cycle assessment is a very in-depth process and may require more technical expertise or time commitment than your business can provide. In this instance, you may decide to hire a consultant to assist you with conducting an LCA. The cost of outsourcing your LCA will vary depending on the nature of the assessment, the availability of existing data, and the number of alternative products you want to compare.

Example: New Leaf Paper

In 1995 New Leaf Paper, with the help of the Environmental Defense Fund and the Paper Task Force, helped to conduct one of the first life cycle assessments for the paper industry. The LCA found that New Leaf Paper customers saved 2.1 million trees, 650 million gallons of water, and 65 million pounds of solid waste from 1998 through 2010 by using New Leaf papers made with an average of 50 percent postconsumer recycled waste.

For additional information on conducting a life cycle assessment of your products, please see the Resources section in the back of the book.

✓ **Monitor and record your greenhouse gas emissions.**

Why Is This on the Assessment?

Greenhouse gases trap heat in the atmosphere. Some GHGs, such as carbon dioxide, are emitted into the atmosphere through natural processes (e.g., volcanic eruptions). Other greenhouse gases are created and emitted solely through human activities.

Because GHG emissions are closely linked to energy usage, calculating your emissions is a great way to identify cost-saving opportunities. Monitoring your GHG emissions also can help you ensure that your company is meeting local regulatory requirements.

How Can You Implement This at Your Company?

Energy Star Portfolio Manager is one of the best free tools to track GHG emissions.[36] Portfolio Manager provides users with the ability to record, track, and communicate the emissions associated with their energy use, and to track the emissions avoided through any green power purchases. In addition, the methodology for calculating greenhouse gas emissions in Portfolio Manager is designed to be consistent and compatible with the accounting, inventory, and reporting requirements of many programs.

Another set of tools, the Greenhouse Gas Protocol, enables companies to develop comprehensive and reliable inventories of their GHG emissions and reflects best practice methods that have been tested by industry experts.[37]

For additional information on monitoring and recording your company's greenhouse gas emissions, please see the Resources section in the back of the book.

INNOVATIVE CHIC. Ditto Hangers, in addition to being made from recycled materials, enable you to fit twice as many clothes in your closet.

✓ **Create a reclamation project to recycle or reuse end products.**

Why Is This Practice Rewarded?

This question rewards companies that accept return of their products for environmentally responsible reuse, recycling, or disposal. Product reclamation is important because many municipalities are not equipped to handle anything beyond the standard paper, glass, plastic, and aluminum.

In response to the challenge of recycling different materials, many countries have started to experiment with extended producer responsibility programs, through which producers are held responsible for the costs of managing their products at the end of their usable life. The theory behind extended producer responsibility is that the producer has the greatest control over the original product design, which gives it the greatest ability and responsibility to deal with its used products.

Example: Preserve

More than one-third of U.S. communities do not accept no. 5 plastics for recycling, meaning that many yogurt cups, medicine bottles, and other no. 5 plastics are sent to landfills or shipped overseas. In response, Preserve created the Gimme 5 program, which offers a simple way to save these plastics and create more opportunities for reuse. Preserve allows customers either to mail in their no. 5 plastics or to recycle them at Gimme 5 bins at more than 250 retail locations across the United States.

Example: Ditto Hangers

Every day an estimated 15.5 million plastic, wire, and wood hangers are dumped into landfills in the United States. Ditto Hangers is addressing this pervasive environmental challenge by designing 100 percent recycled, nontoxic, Forest Stewardship Council-certified hangers that require minimal disassembly and can be recycled in most municipalities. In addition, due to their simple, streamlined design, Ditto's customers can fit twice as many clothes in their closets.

How Can You Implement This at Your Company?

The steps your company must take to implement a reclamation program will largely depend on your industry, location, and company size. The following are some likely steps:

- Research existing programs in your area. The easiest answer may be to partner with an existing industry group or government project.
- Have a discussion with your employees. Your frontline staff often will have the best ideas about potential opportunities for improvement. Try brainstorming a number of ideas and then narrow down your list to the two or three most environmentally beneficial (and feasible) projects.
- Start a small pilot project. It is best to test, adjust, and refine your ideas before launching full-scale reclamation program.
- Seek feedback from a wide range of stakeholders. How did the pilot project work? How can you improve the program's effectiveness? What are the remaining barriers?
- Launch your program. Remember that innovation is a process of continual improvement. Keep experimenting, measuring, and improving your performance.

One of the best ways to learn more is to reach out to some of the Certified B Corps that have product reclamation programs in place. Most B Corps will be happy to share their experiences and to advise you on next steps.

> **Example: Give Something Back Office Supplies**
>
> Give Something Back Office Supplies, a Certified B Corp, operates an electronics recycling program that was originally conceived of by its warehouse employees. GSB's employees noticed that its delivery trucks were full when they left in the morning and empty when they returned in the afternoon. During GSB's B Corp recertification process, employees were asked to contribute their thoughts about how GSB could improve its environmental performance. The warehouse employees suggested that GSB could reduce its carbon footprint and provide a useful service by offering to pick up its customers' old computers, monitors, printers, and other electronic waste.
>
> GSB, which had access to a large volume of e-waste, then partnered with ReliaTech, a social enterprise that dismantles and rebuilds e-waste to create refurbished computers for public schools, low-income families, and nonprofit organizations. ReliaTech also provides technical training and job placement services for low-income, formerly incarcerated, and other chronically underemployed populations.

For additional information on creating a reclamation project to recycle or reuse end products, please see the Resources section in the back of the book.

✓ **Encourage your suppliers to start their own environmental reviews or audits, which may cover energy, water, waste, carbon emissions, renewables, or materials.**

Why Is This Practice Rewarded?

This question rewards companies that help their suppliers improve their social and environmental impact. This question is particularly important because many companies find that the majority of their carbon footprint can be traced back to their supply chains.

One barrier to implementing positive changes, however, is that many of these same businesses lack an easy-to-use, tangible tool to measure, compare, and improve the impact of their individual suppliers. A group of leading companies has started to address this problem by using the B Impact Assessment as a free tool to benchmark their supply chains.

Example: Ben & Jerry's

Ben & Jerry's already sources ingredients from Certified B Corp suppliers such as Coffee Enterprises, Greyston Bakery, and Rhino Foods. As a true social and environmental thought leader, however, Ben & Jerry's is always interested in doing more. The company recently started a pilot project that uses the B Impact Assessment to measure the performance of its supply chain. The objectives of this project include:

- using the B Impact Assessment to measure the performance of a pilot group of Ben & Jerry's suppliers;

- providing Ben & Jerry's with a set of robust, holistic, compelling impact metrics to help demonstrate to key stakeholders the benefits of their values-based sourcing program;

- improved understanding of how the B Impact Assessment can be used to guide Ben & Jerry's sourcing and procurement decisions in the future;

- providing suppliers with the knowledge, resources, and support they need to dramatically improve their social and environmental performance; and

- presenting the pilot project results at conferences and events in order to build brand value and thought leadership.

Ben & Jerry's is now able to use the B Impact Assessment metrics to pinpoint positive (or concerning) areas of supply chain performance by individual suppliers and to identify impact areas that seem to affect suppliers as a group.

Other companies have experimented with providing incentives to increase supplier participation. Incentives can help suppliers take the first step toward improving their performance.

Example: Method

Method's cofounder Adam Lowry describes its supplier incentive program:

Method has been offsetting the carbon footprint for both employee travel and the manufacture of our products since 2004. In 2009 we started to think about a better way to invest that money. Working with carbon offset provider NativeEnergy, we've developed a novel carbon reduction program that emphasizes the primary importance of reducing—rather than just offsetting—our carbon emissions.

The program creates financial incentives for our suppliers to identify the opportunities where we can prevent carbon emissions by partnering with them to find efficiencies and product development and design-side emissions reductions. For any reductions achieved, we shift payments for the offsets that would have been required to the supply chain partner. That's right: we pay our suppliers to reduce their emissions!

B the Change recommendations:

- *Ask your supply chain partners to identify sources of energy efficiency. They'll know their business better than anyone else. You'll be surprised with the results.*

- *Explore carbon offset suppliers that can also help manage and reduce a company's carbon footprint. Remember: reduce, reduce, reduce, then offset.*

- *Look at your whole business—from manufacturing footprint to employee commutes—to see where changes will have the biggest effect.*

How Can You Implement This at Your Company?

There are a few things to consider before engaging your suppliers:

- Conduct pilot initiatives before scaling up. You will probably need a few years of results, data, and feedback before creating a larger program.

- Engage a select number of suppliers that you think would be the most receptive to improving their performance.

- If you are using the B Impact Assessment, explain that it is a free educational tool with best practices, tips, and resources to help them build a better business.
- Assure suppliers that you are collecting data to benchmark the overall impact of your supply chain, not to single out or reprimand suppliers that receive a mixed score on the first try.

For additional information on encouraging your suppliers to start their own environmental reviews or audits, please see the Resources section in the back of the book.

Reflections and Next Steps

Now that you have finished, take a moment to review the previous section, including any answers you gave on the Quick Assessment at the very beginning. Next, take a few minutes to write down your thoughts about the following questions. This will serve as a useful starting point for determining how you will move forward on your journey.

Based on the previous section, what resonates with me/my company?

What changes could we make that would have the greatest positive impact?

What are one or two easy wins?

What are one or two long-term goals?

Moving forward, who are the key players, potential allies, and coleaders?

THE IAN MARTIN GROUP

Tim Masson, CEO,
The Ian Martin Group
RECRUITMENT AND HUMAN RESOURCES
CONSULTING—CANADA

Q: What business benefits do you directly attribute to your B Corp certification?

A: The biggest thing is how other B Corps have given us inspiration to build our culture. For example, our B Corp certification has helped us redefine our values of authenticity, entrepreneurship, and stewardship; engage more people in strategy; and put a premium on learning. As a result, we were listed as one of Canada's fifty best workplaces in 2014 and we have been able to continually attract and retain the best employees in our industry.

Q: What was your biggest surprise about becoming a B Corp?

A: I have been pleasantly surprised with the growing number of old economy businesses joining the B Corp movement. If we're going to make a material change to the way business is done, we need to encourage the millions of established business out there to use business for good, not just the social entrepreneurs or tech start-ups.

Q: How do you plan on using your B Corp certification to add value to your business in the future?

A: As a B2B company, my goal is that we can get other companies (particularly our customers) using a version of the B Impact Assessment to measure their suppliers. Obviously this would benefit us directly, but I think it is one of the biggest levers that could lead to scaling the movement. Once companies can reliably measure the social and environment performance of their suppliers, they will factor this into purchasing decisions, alongside more traditional criteria.

Good for the Long Term

Why this matters: In a word, legacy. You want to build your company on a solid foundation of accountability and transparency so it can retain the values, culture, processes, and high standards you put in place.

Corporate Structure

Transparency

Mission and Engagement

Quick Assessment of Long-Term Impact

Want to get a quick idea of how good your company is for the long term? Take the following twelve-item Quick Assessment to measure your performance over the past year. You can add up your total at the bottom for a rough idea of how you might score on the Governance section of the B Impact Assessment.

Check the box if you and/or your company . . .

Mission and Engagement

☐ integrate a commitment to social and/or environmental responsibility into your written corporate mission statement.

☐ train employees on your social and/or environmental mission.

☐ evaluate employees and management on their performance with regard to your company's social and environmental targets.

☐ tie social and environmental performance to bonuses or other rewards.

☐ solicit from your external stakeholders (e.g., customers, community members, suppliers, or nonprofit organizations) feedback about your company's social and environmental performance.

☐ maintain a board of directors (or other governing body) that meets regularly, has at least one independent outside member, reviews the company's social and environmental performance, and oversees executive compensation.

Transparency

☐ share with your employees basic financial information (e.g., profit and loss statements or balance sheets).

☐ have an open-book management process that allows employees to access all available financial and operational data.

- [ ] produce an external annual report detailing your mission-related performance.

- [ ] work within your industry to develop social and environmental standards.

- [ ] are part of an organization that fosters environmentally sustainable business, fair trade, and/or fair labor practices in your industry.

Corporate Structure

- [ ] have legally institutionalized your mission in your corporate structure (e.g., by inserting a stakeholder consideration into your governing documents or by incorporating as a benefit corporation).

_____ Total

If you scored from **zero to 3,** you will have some work do to earn B Corp certification. Alternatively, you can make up ground with an outstanding performance in the other areas.

If you scored from **4 to 6,** you are a good candidate for B Corp certification, assuming you perform similarly well on the other sections.

If you scored from **7 to 12,** fantastic work! You are likely well on your way to getting the score you need for B Corp certification.

To see how your company stacks up against thousands of other businesses and for more best practice guides and resources, go to **www.bimpactassessment.net.** Don't worry; it's free and confidential.

Yvon Chouinard from Patagonia says he wants to build a company that will last for one hundred years. Steve Voigt from King Arthur Flour says his two-hundred-year-old company became a B Corp so it has a better chance to thrive for another two hundred years. If you are going to build a better business, it is important that it can survive changes in management and ownership.

As we have seen, it can be challenging to build a business that is good for workers, good for the community, and good for the environment. It can be even more challenging to build a business that is good for the long term.

B Corps believe that one of the keys to durability is to bake your mission into your company's cultural and legal DNA. This involves making your mission come to life by increasing shared accountability for your company's long-term success. It means integrating your values into job descriptions, performance reviews, and even your corporate governing documents. It also means being transparent, open, and honest about your company's mission-related performance and how your company can do better in the future.

To help you examine how well your company is positioned for long-term success, the B Impact Assessment focuses on three main areas: mission and engagement, which includes integrating a commitment to sustainability into your mission statement, training employees about your social and environmental values, and soliciting feedback from your stakeholders; transparency, which includes sharing financial information with employees, producing an annual report, and working within your industry to develop social and environmental standards; and corporate structure, which looks at whether your company has institutionalized its mission in its corporate governing documents.

To help you on your journey, I will highlight some of these topics, discuss why they are important, explain why they are rewarded on the assessment, and offer tips for implementing these practices in your company. As with each section, the Quick Assessment section at the start of the chapter and the Reflections and Next Steps section at the end will help you get your bearings and put your new thoughts into action.

✓ **Integrate a commitment to social and/or environmental responsibility into your written corporate mission statement.**

Why Is This Practice Rewarded?

Vision, mission, and values are the foundation of your business. Creating an explicit commitment to social and environmental responsibility can help your business stay purpose-driven, especially through changes in employees, ownership, and management. Many B Corps have found that this is one of the most important things they have done to create internal alignment within their organizations.

How Can You Implement This at Your Company?

If you want to create a vision/mission/values statement for your business, get your board of directors, management team, and employees together and follow the prompts outlined here. Involve as many people as you can.

1. **Vision.** Ask yourself, "What do we want to become?" A vision statement should succinctly describe what your company will look like in five years. For example, "We are nationally recognized as one of the top thought leaders in coaching and strategy for social entrepreneurs."

2. **Mission.** Ask yourself, "What kind of business are we in?" Your mission statement should provide a clear, concise description of your organization's overall purpose. This can enable large groups of individuals to work in a unified direction toward a common cause. A good mission statement should be challenging yet achievable. Patagonia's mission statement, for example, is "Build the best product, cause no unnecessary harm, use business to inspire and implement solutions to the environmental crisis." Method's mission statement is "To inspire a happy and healthy home revolution."

3. **Values.** Ask yourself, "What do we stand for?" The statement of values ties the vision and mission together. It provides the decision-making filter for how the business will conduct its activities while carrying out its mission and vision. For example, Nutiva's values include passion, purity, community, and well-being.

   - Passion: "Nutiva nourishes people and planet, taking pride in our growing family of food products."
   - Purity: "Nutiva delivers certified organic superfoods that surpass customer expectations."

- Community: "Nutiva is dedicated to a healthy and sustainable world for all."
- Well-being: "Nutiva supports the idea that health is our greatest wealth."

✓ **Train employees on your social and/or environmental mission.**

Why Is This Practice Rewarded?

Providing formal training about your social and/or environmental mission can help motivate and engage your employees by connecting them to the purpose behind your corporate objectives.

> *The number one thing we do to encourage employee engagement is take teammates on a trip to the rain forest to be a part of harvest in an indigenous community. About half of our forty-five people have been there, and several of our teammates are based full time in Argentina or Paraguay. This really keeps everyone connected to the mission and vision and continues to inspire positivity across the company.*
>
> Chris Mann, CEO, Guayaki
> TEA AND BEVERAGES—CALIFORNIA

How Can You Implement This at Your Company?

Start by explaining your company's social and environmental goals to all new hires. Embed these goals in the employee handbook. Next, create training for all employees on your social mission. Ask one of your long-term employees, board members, or investors to give a presentation about how your company's mission aims to solve social or environmental challenges. For example, King Arthur Flour hosts ESOP 101, which explains employee ownership, why King Arthur Flour is employee owned, and how employees can become eligible to participate in the employee stock ownership plan.

One of the best ways to connect your employees to your values is to give them firsthand experience. For example, United By Blue's mission is to raise awareness about plastic pollution in the ocean. Although its core business is selling clothing made from recycled ocean plastics, the company also organizes river and beach cleanups that give employees a personal connection to the problem of plastic waste. All employees at United By Blue are encouraged to either attend or lead a cleanup as a step toward better understanding of the company's mission.

> *The B Impact Assessment motivated us to create a new position in the company—a mission manager—dedicated entirely to managing our social and environmental impact and keeping us on track as a responsible business. Having one person continually guarding and representing our commitment to all stakeholders has allowed us to really amplify our commitment to being a better business.*
>
> Victoria Fiore, Mission Manager, Plum Organics
> HEALTHY CHILDREN'S SNACKS—CALIFORNIA

✓ **Evaluate employees and management on their performance with regard to the company's social and environmental targets. Consider tying social and environmental performance to bonuses or other rewards.**

Why Is This Practice Rewarded?

Are your employees and managers evaluated using written, predetermined social and environmental goals? If not, consider integrating these into your annual performance reviews. Creating accountability (and more incentives) for meeting social and environmental goals can increase employee engagement in your sustainability initiatives.

Example: Seventh Generation

Seventh Generation has excelled at creating a shared employee understanding of its culture of sustainability. Seventh Generation's employee engagement program, LEAD (Learn, Engage, Act, and Demonstrate), provides employees with an opportunity to learn about and take action on environmental and social issues relevant to its business. Seventh Generation has tied the goal of 100 percent employee participation in LEAD to its annual incentive program.

How Can You Implement This at Your Company?

Have a conversation with your employees about their performance reviews. Tell them why you are considering specific social and environmental goals and how this aligns with your company's values. Explaining the purpose behind the proposed changes, and allowing your employees to have a say in the process, will be much more effective than forced compliance.

One of the best ways to generate employee sustainability targets is to take the B Impact Assessment. This can help spark a wide variety of ideas, such as turning off lights that are not in use, biking to work at least once a week, organizing a carpool group, or recycling/composting whenever possible.

> *The assessment tool continues to be a valuable guidance on best practices—across all of our operations—by demonstrating how to put our values into practice. For example, we knew we wanted employees to grow personally and professionally, and we wanted to be able to better recognize employee accomplishments. Through the B Impact Assessment we identified improvements to our annual performance review that could help us support employee growth and engagement. As a result, we've created a specific company goal to create infrastructure and processes that will add characteristics like peer and subordinate input, written guidance for career development, and social and environmental targets to our annual review.*

> Danielle Cresswell, Director of Sustainability, Klean Kanteen
> REUSABLE FOOD AND BEVERAGE CONTAINERS—CALIFORNIA

For additional information on evaluating employee and management performance with regard to the company's social and environmental targets, please see the Resources section in the back of the book.

✓ **Solicit from your external stakeholders (e.g., customers, community members, suppliers, or nonprofit organizations) feedback about your company's social and environmental performance.**

Why Is This Practice Rewarded?

This question rewards businesses that have a formal, structured process to solicit feedback about the company's social and environmental impact. This practice is encouraged because stakeholders often are greatly affected by a company's decisions but usually have no say in the decision-making process. General customer satisfaction or product feedback, while important on its own, is not rewarded in this context.

How Can You Implement This at Your Company?

One of the best ways to generate new ideas about improving your performance is to ask the people who engage with your company on a regular basis. For example, try creating a specific social and environmental feedback section on your website, sending out an online survey, or creating a contest and giving out prizes. Start with your top five suppliers and/or your best customers. Use their feedback to refine and improve your practices.

> ### Example: Sustainable Harvest
>
> Sustainable Harvest invites its stakeholders, including farmers, processors, and baristas, to an annual event called Let's Talk Coffee. This event provides the much-needed space for small-scale farmers to discuss important issues such as fair pricing, worker treatment, and quality standards that respect the environment.

✓ **Maintain a board of directors (or other governing body) that meets regularly, has at least one independent member, reviews the company's social and environmental performance, and oversees executive compensation.**

Why Is This Practice Rewarded?

This question rewards companies that have a governing body that, in addition to reviewing sales and operations, also audits financials, oversees executive compensation, and reviews the company's social and environmental performance. In addition, governing bodies that include employees (i.e., nonexecutive management), community members, and/or environmental experts also are rewarded, because their insights and expertise can help ensure that the company makes decisions that benefit all of its stakeholders.

> ### Example: Blue Avocado
>
> The board of directors of Blue Avocado, a company that sells eco-friendly reusable bags, reviews the company's social and environmental performance in several areas. For example, the board reviews the amount by which carbon emissions are reduced through the sales of its bags, the environmental footprint of its manufacturing partners, and the number of microloans the company awards each year.

How Can You Implement This at Your Company?

Encourage employees, community members, and environmental experts to apply for a board seat. The following are some examples of questions to ask prospective board members:

- What interests you about our organization and our cause?
- What motivates you to volunteer?
- What personal or professional goals do you have that could be advanced by service on our board?
- Do you anticipate any constraints on your time?
- What skills, connections, resources, and expertise could you offer our organization?
- Do you have any worries about joining the board?
- What do you need from us to make your board experience as successful as possible?

For additional information on maintaining an effective board of directors or other governing body, please see the Resources section in the back of the book.

✓ **Consider sharing financial and operational information with your employees.**

Why Is This Practice Rewarded?

Transparency builds trust. Trust is the foundation of strong relationships. And your relationship with your employees is one of your most important assets.

This question rewards companies that are transparent about their finances. The level of transparency ranges from sharing basic revenue figures to disclosing all available financial information (e.g., profit and loss statements, balance sheets, and/or salary information). Sharing finances may include, for example, distributing information directly to employees or sharing information during a presentation.

In addition, some companies have an open-book management process that enables employees to access real-time financial and operational data. An open-book program can contribute to the overall success of the company by empowering employees and departments to set and maintain their own financial goals.

How Can You Implement This at Your Company?

This is a very personal decision for every company. If you currently do not share any financial information, I would suggest sharing with your employees at least basic financial figures, such as core revenue sources and operational costs, on a regular basis.

In addition to sharing information, it can be mutually beneficial to teach employees why certain financial and operational data is valuable. For example, if you make a product, consider sharing trends, such as which product lines are growing in revenue or margin. Explain the underlying assumptions of your financial projections. You also should be transparent about unresolved challenges (e.g., "We see an opportunity to reduce costs on our new product line, but we are not sure about our next steps."). This is an opportunity to motivate and engage your employees by helping them learn about new areas of the business.

SOUTHERNENERGY
MANAGEMENT

Maria Kingery, Cofounder and CEO, Southern Energy Management
SOLAR ENERGY—NORTH CAROLINA

Q: What business benefits do you directly attribute to your B Corp certification?

A: Our B Corp certification has enabled us to qualify and quantify the impact we are working to create in the world, and to communicate that clearly to our customers. We also became part of a community of businesses that share our values. We've met some amazing people and formed some outstanding business relationships that I don't believe would have come about without the B Corp connection.

Q: What was the biggest challenge you had to overcome to certify as a B Corp?

A: Convincing our leadership team that it was a good idea. They were skeptical at first, but the companies who were already on board inspired them. In the end they were convinced that twenty-five years from now this is just how business is going to be done, and we'll get to say that we helped make that happen.

Q: If you could change one thing about the B Corp movement, what would it be?

A: I believe the B Corp movement could really benefit (pun intended) from a more intentional business development focus for its members. We all have similar challenges (and opportunities!), and it would be great to work through some of those together. Here in North Carolina, we've made some efforts to build our community, and that's been somewhat successful, but really, there's so much more we could be doing to help and learn from each other.

> ### Example: New Belgium Brewing Company
>
> New Belgium Brewing Company has an open-book management program that encourages fiscal transparency, communication, and innovation. For example:
>
> - all new hires learn basic financial concepts and tools during orientation;
> - managers share department finances with their teams on a routine basis;
> - monthly all-staff sessions are convened to discuss business performance and to enable employees to ask questions;
> - remote employees participate in online forums to engage with decision makers and learn about the latest business trends; and
> - employees access a variety of information from the company intranet, which provides financials, dashboard metrics with progress updates, and a means to interact with other employees and managers.
>
> New Belgium's open-book management also fosters employee engagement and creativity, which in turn drives the company's sustainability efforts. For example, two New Belgium employees recently proposed eliminating twelve-bottle pack dividers, which saved the company more than $280,000, reduced paper waste by 150 tons, and reduced machine downtime.
>
> Anne C. Broughton and Jessica Thomas, *Embracing Open-Book Management to Fuel Employee Engagement and Corporate Sustainability* (Chapel Hill, NC: UNC Kenan–Flagler Business School, 2012).

✓ **Produce an external annual report detailing your mission-related performance.**

Why Is This Practice Rewarded?

Just as sharing financials can help build employee trust, sharing your mission-related performance with the public can help build consumer and local community trust. Producing an annual report is one of many ways to help show that your company is making progress toward its mission.

The process of creating an annual report can be very beneficial for your company. Some companies find that the process of compiling the information helps them uncover social and environmental risks, inefficiencies, and opportunities that otherwise would have gone unnoticed. This process can also be a helpful means of building consensus and accountability systems internally to better track your company's performance over time.

How Can You Implement This at Your Company?

If your company has never produced a mission-related report, the following are a few questions to consider:

- Do you have clear descriptions of your mission-related activities?
- Have you identified the positive and negative effects of your company's operations on society and the environment?
- Can you prepare quantifiable targets and results related to your mission (e.g., pounds of carbon offset)?
- Can you report with consistent variables of measurement, which will allow comparisons to previous years or other businesses?
- Have you solicited feedback from your various stakeholder groups to help determine which information to report?
- Is there third-party validation of the contents of your report?

If you would like a comprehensive, straightforward, and free tool to help you create a mission-related report, I encourage you to benchmark your company's performance by using the B Impact Assessment.

Each year we have an independent auditor compare our B Impact Assessment score with our operations and make recommendations for ways we can make a bigger positive difference. Although we've run a purpose-centered business model for a long time, the assessment continues to expand our thinking and push us to consider new ways we can improve our efforts to serve.

Kevin Trapani, CEO, The Redwoods Group
INSURANCE SERVICES—NORTH CAROLINA

For additional information on producing an external annual report detailing your mission-related performance, please see the Resources section in the back of the book.

✓ **Work within your industry to develop social and environmental standards. Join an organization that fosters environmentally sustainable business, fair trade, and/or fair labor practices in your industry.**

Why Is This Practice Rewarded?

In addition to rewarding individual improvements, the B Impact Assessment acknowledges businesses that advocate reforms in their industry. There often are stronger commitments and higher rates of adoption when change is led by businesses within a certain sector.

There are many ways that you can improve your industry's overall social and environmental performance. For example, you could serve on a working group to help educate your peers, advocate the adoption of voluntary environmental reporting standards, or help pass legislation that creates incentives for businesses to improve their performance.

How Can You Implement This at Your Company?

Research the various trade associations in your sector. There is a good chance that there are already some social and environmental initiatives within your industry. Contact other businesses and try to get involved. If there is no existing sustainability initiative, try to start one.

Another excellent step would be to get involved with existing organizations that promote social and environmental responsibility. Examples include the American Sustainable Business Council, the Business Alliance for Local Living Economies, Green America, the Green Chamber of Commerce, the Fair Labor Association, Fairtrade International, and Social Venture Network.

Example: One Step Closer
to an Organic Sustainable Solution

A coalition of businesses in the natural foods industry, including B Corporations such as Alter Eco, Guayaki, Numi Organic Tea, Plum Organics, and Traditional Medicinals, have come together to form a group called One Step Closer to an Organic Sustainable Solution (OSC^2). The members of OSC^2 are using open collaboration, innovation, and their collective purchasing power to reduce the amount of waste created by packaged consumer goods.

Example: Sustainable Apparel Coalition

The Sustainable Apparel Coalition, originally started by Patagonia, is a trade organization comprising brands, retailers, manufacturers, government, nongovernment organizations, and academic experts, representing more than one-third of the global apparel and footwear market. The coalition is working to reduce the environmental and social impacts of apparel and footwear products around the world. The organization's vision and purpose are based on the shared belief that:

- environmental and social challenges related to the global apparel supply system affect the entire industry;

- these challenges reflect systemic issues that no individual company can solve on its own;

- precompetitive collaboration can accelerate improvement in environmental and social performance for the industry as a whole and can reduce cost for individual companies;

- this collaboration enables individual companies to focus more resources on product and process innovation; and

- credible, practical, and universal standards and tools for defining and measuring environmental and social performance support the individual interests of all stakeholders.

✓ **Legally institutionalize your mission in your corporate governing documents.**

Why Is This Practice Rewarded?

If your company is good for workers, good for communities, and good for the environment, then it is important that your company's mission is protected for the long term. One of the best ways to protect your mission is to embed your company's core social and environmental values in your corporate governing documents—the legal DNA of your business. By elevating your values to the status of law, your company will be able to maintain its mission through changes in management and ownership. This practice is rewarded because the consideration of stakeholder interests in corporate decision making is a simple yet radical shift in the evolution of capitalism.

B Corp enshrines Patagonia's nearly fifty-year-old model of business into law, and that makes it easier for other businesses to adopt this model and use it in their own search for stewardship and sustainability.

Rick Ridgeway, Vice President of Environmental Initiatives, Patagonia
OUTDOOR APPAREL—CALIFORNIA

How Can You Implement This at Your Company?

The process of institutionalizing stakeholder interests into your governing documents is dependent on your location (e.g., whether your company is incorporated in the United States) and your existing legal structure (e.g., limited liability company, corporation, or partnership). It is outside the scope of this discussion to explain the legal process in detail. Therefore, I highly recommend contacting a legal expert such as Bill Clark from Drinker Biddle & Reath; Donald Simon from Wendel, Rosen, Black & Dean; or Jonathan Storper from Hanson Bridgett. In addition, the appendix contains information about the differences between Certified B Corporations and benefit corporations.[38]

 **VERIS** Wealth Partners

Anders Ferguson, Partner, Veris Wealth Partners
IMPACT INVESTING—NEW YORK

Q: What business benefits do you directly attribute to your B Corp certification?

A: One of the toughest parts of being a financial advisor is working to characterize the impacts from our clients' investments. Thanks to the B Corp certification and the B Analytics framework, we have, for the first time, tools to rate impact in our private equity and debt investments. This is a major advance.

Q: What was your biggest surprise about becoming a B Corp?

A: We were surprised at what a big difference it means to our firm, employees, clients, business partners, and more. We wanted to do the right thing, but this opens up doors you couldn't have predicted. Certification has been an incredible morale booster, it is something that nonfinancial friends and family can understand, and it also encourages our own independent personal behaviors.

Q: What advice do you have for a business that is considering B Corp certification?

A: Remember that B Corp certification is not prescriptive—there is no "right" way to score or be as a company; there is only your company's way, which is made up of a series of decisions and actions made by your company's employees. Consider and ponder a bit. Make preparations. But then just get on with it and get certified. It's a process. It unfolds as you go. Until you take the first step or leap and get certified, frankly, it's all kind of an intellectual analysis.

Reflections and Next Steps

Now that you have finished, take a moment to review the previous section, including any answers you gave on the Quick Assessment at the very beginning. Next, take a few minutes to write down your thoughts about the following questions. This will serve as a useful starting point for determining how you will move forward on your journey.

Based on the previous section, what resonates with me/my company?

What changes could we make that would have the greatest positive impact?

What are one or two easy wins?

What are one or two long-term goals?

Moving forward, who are the key players, potential allies, and coleaders?

Good to
the Core

Why this matters: Everything starts with intention. What problems could your business help address if it were designed to do so from the start?

Restore the Environment

Strengthen Communities

Serve Those in Need

Create Broad Ownership

Quick Assessment of Core Impact

This Quick Assessment looks at your company's core business model and rewards companies that use particularly innovative means of solving social and environmental problems.

Check the box if you and/or your company . . .

☐ provide one or more of the following: health care or healthy products; education; support for the arts or cultural heritage; improved social and economic empowerment; access to markets through previously unavailable infrastructure; or support for purpose-driven organizations through fundraising, capital, and/or capacity building.

☐ benefit the environment through one or more of the following: renewable or clean energy; improved energy and/or water efficiency; reduced waste; conserving land or wildlife; reducing toxic chemicals and hazardous substances; pollution prevention and remediation methods; measuring, researching, or providing information to solve environmental problems; providing financing and/or lending tied to an environmental mission.

☐ are at least 40 percent owned by workers (e.g., a worker cooperative).

☐ are a producer cooperative in which owners are supplier members who organize production (e.g., a farmer or artisanal cooperative).

☐ focus on alleviating poverty through your supply chain by sourcing through fair wage–certified suppliers; provide technical assistance and/or capacity building to small-scale suppliers (e.g., individuals, cooperatives, or companies with fewer than fifty workers); or use contracts to guarantee future purchases and payments to suppliers.

☐ use a microfranchising or microdistribution model. Microfranchises, on average, have fewer than ten workers, are independently owned and operated, and distribute products exclusively for the parent company. Microdistribution is a sales and revenue model that relies on a network of individual sellers or retailers for whom the product represents at least 50 percent of their total income.

- [ ] donate at least 20 percent of profits or 2 percent of sales to charity or a non-profit foundation annually, or are at least 20 percent owned by a nonprofit.

- [ ] target and hire more than 10 percent of total workers from chronically under-employed populations (e.g., low-income or formerly incarcerated people) and/or extensively train and invest in these workers.

- [ ] are specifically designed to rebuild the local community.

- [ ] have production practices that are designed to conserve the environment across the company's entire operation (e.g., retrofitting facilities to make them more energy efficient; changing your transport and distribution practices; or monitoring, recording, and reducing energy, waste, and emissions).

_____ Total

If you scored **zero points** in this section, you probably have some work do to earn B Corp certification. Alternatively, you can make up ground with an outstanding performance in the other areas.

If you scored **1 point** in this section, you are still a good candidate for B Corp certification, due to the high value of the questions in this section.

If you scored **2 points or more,** fantastic work! Due to the high value of these questions, you are likely well on your way to getting the score you need for B Corp certification.

To see how your company stacks up against thousands of other businesses and for more best practice guides and resources, go to **www.bimpactassessment.net.** Don't worry; it's free and confidential.

I ntention is a very powerful force. William McDonough, the world-class architect, designer, and coauthor of the seminal book *Cradle to Cradle*, says that "design is a signal of intention."[39] In green building, for example, McDonough argues that we should design buildings that improve human health, improve water quality, absorb carbon dioxide, and release fresh oxygen into the atmosphere, not just design buildings that minimize harm. McDonough's point is that it takes a different starting point, or a different level of intention, to address our most challenging problems.

The Impact Business Models section of the B Impact Assessment was created to recognize and reward that same intention in designing a business. For example, Give Something Back Office Supplies is a Certified B Corp that was founded with the intention of selling a commodity that we all need—office supplies—and then donating a majority of its profits back to local charities. The incredibly large, positive effect that Give Something Back has on its local community reflects the level of intention that was designed into the company from the start.

DESIGN/BUILD FOR GOOD. Échale! a Tu Casa helps low-income families build their own homes.

If you look at the Quick Assessment at the beginning of this section, you will see that the Impact Business Models portion of the B Impact Assessment is incredibly broad. To keep this book focused and to provide the most value to the majority of readers, I have included only two Impact Business Model questions to evaluate in detail here. The best way to learn more about the entire Impact Business Models section is to look at the B Impact Assessment.[40]

✓ **Provide products and/or services that benefit underserved communities.**

Why Is This Practice Rewarded?

This section acknowledges businesses that have designed their core products, services, or processes to help disadvantaged or underserved communities.

Example: Échale! a Tu Casa

Échale! a Tu Casa ("Check In! to Your Home") is a B Corp that operates in the Campeche region of Mexico. The average family in Campeche lives in a hut constructed of plastic tarps and scrap sheet metal. Even if the families in Campeche could afford new homes, the lottery line to obtain a home through a private contractor or the local government can be as long as fourteen years.

Échale! a Tu Casa teaches these families how to build their own homes. The company coordinates design and assembly, and the families construct the home with the help of the company's expert engineers.

Échale! a Tu Casa has intentionally designed its homes so that more than 60 percent of materials can be made or sourced locally, which avoids the need for more-expensive imported building materials. This business model reduces the labor and materials costs so that each family needs to borrow as little as possible.

How Can You Implement This at Your Company?

There is no standard formula for creating products or services that benefit underserved communities. To learn more, I recommend reaching out to some of the existing B Corporations that have created innovative business models in this area.

If you are thinking of creating a product or service for impoverished communities, the following are some general principles your team should consider:

- Focus on radical product redesign from the beginning. Marginal changes to existing products designed for use in developed countries are much less likely to work.

- Products must perform in hostile environments with noise, dust, unsanitary conditions, electrical blackouts, or water pollution.

- Try hybrid solutions, such as blending an old and a new technology.

- Create scalable, transportable operations across countries, cultures, and languages.

- Reduce resource intensity. Create eco-friendly products.

- Identify ways to teach people without formal education to use your product.

- Think about an adaptable user interface for heterogeneous consumer bases.

- Design distribution methods to reach both widely dispersed rural markets and extremely dense urban markets.

- Enable quick and easy incorporation of new features.[41]

✓ **Help lift suppliers and producers out of poverty through fair trade practices. Help your suppliers become cooperative owners of their businesses.**

Why Is This Practice Rewarded?

One of the steps that can dramatically benefit your suppliers is to ensure that basic human rights and wage standards are met in your overseas factories. The concept of fair trade has emerged as a way to verify and promote these practices in your supply chain. According to Fair Trade USA, some of the principles of fair trade include fair wages, inclusive participation, transparency, a focus on training and capacity building, and long-term relationships.[42]

- **Fair wages.** All workers should earn a wage that is adequate to support a family and includes an additional "premium" that will enable the community to build infrastructure such as schools, to ensure access to clean water, and to undertake other projects.

- **Inclusive participation and transparency.** Producers should be empowered to join together in democratically governed associations that give all producers a voice in price, quality, logistics, and general community decisions.

- **Focus on training and capacity building.** Resources should be in place to enable producers to advance their skills through professional training. This training may cover topics such as workplace safety, freedom of association, freedom from discrimination, financial management, pricing and international market mechanisms, or environmental conservation.

- **Long-term relationships.** Fair trade emphasizes long-term relationships rather than short-term, price-oriented sourcing decisions. Long-term contracts with suppliers enable producers to plan their production or farming cycles with more reliability and makes it far easier to secure necessary financing.

The B Impact Assessment rewards companies that adhere to fair trade principles, because these principles allow producers to focus on building wealth instead of struggling to survive. Fair trade practices now reach about 1.2 million farmers in seventy countries and are represented by more than twelve thousand products in the United States.

Mightybytes

Tim Frick, Principal,
Mightybytes
WEB AND MEDIA SERVICES—ILLINOIS

Q: What business benefits do you directly attribute to your B Corp certification?

A: What has been such a remarkable thing about the certification process is that it provides a great framework for continuing to improve over time. There's always a low score you can improve upon. We regularly revisit what being a B Corp means to Mightybytes and encourage our entire team to devise fun ideas that embody the spirit of B Corp while also helping us be a better company.

Q: What was your biggest surprise about becoming a B Corp?

A: Immediately after our first certification (we've since recertified) we reached out blindly to a few other B Corps and were pleasantly surprised at how welcoming they were. We had no idea how strong and powerful the idea of neighborly sharing was within the B Corp community until those initial cold calls. It's something we really appreciate.

There's really no such thing as a "sales call" in the traditional sense of the word when it comes to talking to other B Corps, because you often spend more time talking about what each company is doing within the community and how you're working toward being a better company than you do actually selling your products or services. This builds trust, which in turn drives ideas, which leads to innovation and sharing, which builds community, which generates leads and referrals. Everyone wins.

FAIR TRADE. Through fair trade and ethical practices, Ouro Verde Amazonia benefits local indigenous communities, reduces deforestation, and ensures the availability of healthy superfoods to its customers.

A handful of B Corps have become supplier-owned cooperatives, meaning that the producers are also the owners of the company. These cooperatives provide services such as co-packing, distribution, and sales that the producers would otherwise have to do on their own. In some cases, producers also take raw ingredients and turn them into value-added products. For example, Cabot Creamery's cooperative member farms provide raw milk that the company turns into cheeses, butter, and other dairy products.

Although farmers' cooperatives have existed for a long time, modern cooperatives combine the principles of fair trade with a democratic structure to dramatically improve economic opportunity for producers.

Example: Pachamama Coffee Farmers

Pachamama Coffee Farmers, fondly referred to as Pacha, is a cooperative owned by 113,000 farming families in Ethiopia, Guatemala, Mexico,
Nicaragua, and Peru. Pacha manages the farmers' sales and distribution
relationships with large retailers, restaurants, universities, and hospitals
in North America, which provides a steady income for each of its individual farmer–owners. In addition, Pacha benefits the environment by
using its collective strength to spread more sustainable coffee-growing
and processing practices.

How Can You Implement This at Your Company?

Talk to your current suppliers about fair trade principles. See whether they have
ever considered cooperative ownership or third-party certification to verify their
social and environmental practices. If not, try asking them to take the B Impact
Assessment. When your suppliers start to see the different steps they can take,
they may be willing to have a conversation about fair trade and/or cooperative
ownership.

For additional information on fair trade practices and helping your suppliers
become cooperative owners of their businesses, please see the Resources section
in the back of the book.

Reflections and Next Steps

Now that you have finished, take a moment to review the previous section, including any answers you gave on the Quick Assessment at the very beginning. Next,
take a few minutes to write down your thoughts about the following questions.
This will serve as a useful starting point for determining how you will move forward on your journey.

Based on the previous section, what resonates with me/my company?

What changes could we make that would have the greatest positive impact?

What are one or two easy wins?

What are one or two long-term goals?

Moving forward, who are the key players, potential allies, and coleaders?

Kevin Trapani, CEO,
The Redwoods Group
INSURANCE SERVICES—NORTH CAROLINA

Q: How do you leverage your B Corp status in your branding/ marketing?

A: We use it in our messaging quite a bit. Our business is built on being a different kind of insurance provider—one that works with you to prevent bad things from happening on the front end but is there for you as a partner when something does go wrong. Sharing that we're a Certified B Corporation helps prove that we're not just telling you we're different; we live out a different business model every day.

Q: What business benefits do you directly attribute to your B Corp certification?

A: The certification provides us with positive competitive differentiation. We only serve nonprofit customers, so B Corp Certification proves we share their mission of making a positive difference. It has helped us maintain our customer relationships even in the face of much-lower-cost options.

It's also been a very powerful recruitment and retention tool, as we've found that our best people want to be a part of something bigger. Being a B Corp proves that we're the right place for them.

Q: What advice do you have for a business considering B Corp certification?

A: If you're a purpose-centered business, this is a great way to distinguish yourself and build the movement of companies who are committed to the greater good and live that commitment every day.

4

The Quick Start Guide

Getting Started

Welcome to the six-week, turbocharged Quick Start Guide. This section is designed both for businesses that want to become a Certified B Corporation and for businesses that are unsure about B Corp certification but want a straightforward, step-by-step road map to help them measure, compare, and improve their social and environmental performance.

If you are unsure about whether B Corp certification is right for you, feel free to do as much (or as little) of the following section as you wish. This six-week guide can be seen as an informal resource to help you plan and implement improvements to your business.

Those who are ready to become a Certified B Corporation should follow the same six-week, step-by-step guide, but there are a few extra steps you will need to complete to meet the minimum requirements for B Corp certification. These extra steps are marked "B Corps only" in each weekly segment.

Whether you are seeking B Corp certification or not, the size and complexity of your company will affect how quickly you can move through the following section. For example, smaller companies—especially service companies or companies without outside investors—should be able to move through the Quick Start Guide in less than six weeks. Larger companies with a sizable number of employees and/or departments will probably need the full six weeks or more.

Finally, you will have the best chance of successfully completing this process if:

- you have the ability to see that "the perfect is the enemy of the good." If you try to be perfect on the B Impact Assessment, you run the risk of getting bogged down and never finishing. Aim for good enough and continue to improve your score in the future.

- you or someone else in your company "owns" the project. If many people are working on a project, it often means that no one is actually responsible for moving it forward. Make sure that someone (whether it is you, an external consultant, or another employee) has taken ownership of the project and will dedicate the time and energy necessary to see it through to completion.

- you have access to financial, worker, supplier, community, and environmental data. If you don't personally have access to this data, you need access to the people who are responsible for this data (e.g., the facility manager for energy usage or the human resources manager for employee metrics).

Do not automatically assume that planning for six weeks is too aggressive to complete this process. Try keeping everything to a tight schedule and adjust as needed. You might be surprised at how much you can get done in a short time.

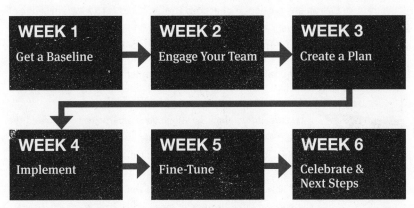

SIX WEEKS TO A BETTER BUSINESS. Follow this step-by-step guide to improve your business in six weeks or less.

Week 1
Get a Baseline

Time estimate: Ninety minutes.

OBJECTIVE: The objective during week 1 is to use the B Impact Assessment to establish a quick baseline of your company's overall social and environmental performance and to create momentum before engaging others in the process.

END RESULT: A rough B Impact Report for your company.

☐ **Clear your schedule.** Clear an uninterrupted ninety-minute slot on your calendar. If it is too difficult to set aside one block of time, consider three thirty-minute slots. The point is that you need some focused time.

☐ **Create your B Impact Assessment account.** Create your free account online at bimpactassessment.net. As you register, you will be asked questions about your company's size, industry, and location in order to generate a version of the assessment that is tailored to fit your business. For example, a marketing company with six employees will get different questions than a furniture manufacturer with six thousand employees.

☐ **Ready, set, go!** Begin working through the assessment. Remember, on this first attempt, to estimate your answers and to avoid spending more than a minute or two on any particular question. The goal is to get a rough baseline of your practices in ninety minutes or less. There are five sections: Governance, Workers, Community, Environment, and Impact Business Models. If you don't make it through all five in ninety minutes, don't worry. Clear another thirty minutes on your calendar later in the week to complete what is left.

RYAN'S TIP If you are unsure about how to answer a particular question in the online assessment, you can check the Revisit This box and skip it. Don't dig up specific data or e-mail or call anyone until you have finished your initial pass through. At the end of the assessment, you can run a Revisit This report that enables you to see all of the questions you guessed on, estimated, or didn't know how to answer. Use this report to create a single, comprehensive e-mail for each person from whom you need information (e.g., your accountant, human resources person, or facilities manager). This approach is a much more effective use of everyone's time and energy.

- [ ] **Review your preliminary score.** At the end of your first trial run, you will receive a baseline B Impact Report that will give you a snapshot of your company's overall social and environmental performance. This report will also contain benchmarks so that you can compare your performance to more than fifteen thousand other businesses that have completed the assessment.

- [ ] **Did you score 40 to 60?** An overall B Impact Score of 40 to 60 is average. This means you've got a solid foundation on which to build. The fun part will be working with your colleagues to determine which impact areas (i.e., governance, workers, community, or environment) you want to improve.

- [ ] **Did you score 60 to 80?** If you received an overall B Impact Score of 60 or higher, nice work! It sounds like your company has already adopted quite a few socially and environmentally responsible practices. From here, your goal will be to help mobilize your team to improve your performance in the areas that matter most to you and your company.

- [ ] **Did you score 80 or higher?** If you received an overall B Impact Score of 80 or higher, congratulations! Eighty is the minimum score necessary for B Corp certification. If you are interested, I highly recommend that you consider pursuing B Corp certification to give your company the recognition it deserves.

- [ ] **Regardless of your initial overall score, remember that this is a journey of continuous improvement.** Are there areas you and others in your company should be proud of? Are there areas you would like to work on? This will give you a few things to think about as you move forward into week 2.

Week 2
Engage Your Team

Time Estimate: Ninety minutes.

OBJECTIVE: The objective during week 2 is to identify coworkers who may be interested in helping you use your business as a force for good. During this week you will have a chance to get different people involved and to get help answering any questions that you marked "revisit."

END RESULT: An informal working group to help you update your B Impact Report with more accurate information.

☐ **Set up a summit with key internal stakeholders.** The first step to securing early buy-in and building project momentum is to organize a larger meeting with the key people in your company. The invite list for this meeting might include, for example, your CEO, CFO, COO, sustainability director, marketing director, human resources manager, or building manager. If you are in the manufacturing or wholesale sectors, you may wish to include key individuals from the product design, sourcing, and supply chain divisions. You want the decision makers in the room to get everyone up to speed. This will help you build momentum as the project moves forward.

☐ **Explain the objectives and benefits.** Explain what you are trying to achieve, what you think success would look like, and how this project will benefit the company. For example, you could say, "There is a big opportunity to use our business as a force for good, and we need your help figuring out how to drive our company toward this vision." It can help to tailor your presentation based on who is attending the meeting, because certain objectives, metrics of success, and benefits will appeal to particular executives. For example:

- the CEO wants to attract and retain the best talent;
- the CFO wants to attract investors and/or save money;
- human resources wants to motivate and engage employees;
- the marketing team may want to generate press, join a national ad campaign, or benefit from a trusted third-party standard;
- the sales team wants to increase consumer trust and/or create partnerships with other mission-aligned businesses;
- operations managers want to save money through operational efficiency;

- sustainability managers want to benchmark performance, share best practices, or earn recognition; and

- everyone wants a network with high-performing peers.

☐ **Share the assessment process and results.** Explain that you have already kick-started your company's journey by completing a baseline and generating a preliminary score. Share what you have learned through the B Impact Report, the best practice examples, and any relevant case studies. Invite a discussion about the opportunities for the company. What matters most to different individuals? What matters most to the team? What are the biggest strengths and weaknesses? Use the Reflections and Next Steps worksheets from part 3 to help guide your discussion.

☐ **Identify a core project team.** Although there may be a wide variety of internal stakeholders at this meeting, you should try to identify a core project team that can help you dig into the details, create an improvement plan, and implement any changes. This project team may or may not include your management team. Line managers, associates, interns, and even board members can be a huge support in helping to turn ideas into action.

RYAN'S TIP — When creating a project team, choose passion over seniority. For example, a highly motivated associate can be a more effective teammate than an uninspired CFO. Although you want senior-level buy-in, this does not mean that every senior executive needs to help with project execution.

☐ **Set clear next steps.** Set up a meeting with your core project team. The goal of this meeting will be to start moving forward with the data collection and implementation process.

☐ **Start discussing the B Corp legal framework (B Corps only).** Discuss with key board members, legal counsel, and investors why it is important to maintain the company's mission over the long term. B Lab has compiled a great set of materials to help you answer questions that your investors or board members are likely to ask.[1]

Week 3
Create a Plan

Time estimate: One to three hours.

OBJECTIVE: After you have identified your core project team, work with them to set a target B Impact Score and create an action plan with short-, medium-, and long-term goals. For example, if you started out with a score of 53, see whether you can implement enough practices to earn an additional ten points by the end of this six-week Quick Start Guide.

END RESULT: An action plan with specific people assigned to take the lead on each question, a target B Impact Score, and a rough timeline for completion.

☐ **Use the improvement tools.** Show your team the Improve Your Impact section of the B Impact Assessment. This will contain your Revisit This report, to help them see which questions you marked for follow-up on your initial pass; a customized improvement report, which will help you decide where you want to focus your efforts (based on impact area, question difficulty, and question weighting); and a library of best practice guides, which will provide more detailed instructions on implementing certain practices.[2]

☐ **Prioritize by difficulty.** You can organize the data in the improvement report in many different ways. Initially, I suggest sorting the questions based on difficulty. Make a plan to tackle the easy and medium-difficulty questions first. Figure out what kind of data you need in order to make progress on the assessment.

> **RYAN'S TIP** I encourage you to use the [online] Improve Your Impact report to identify the point value of the different questions on the B Impact Assessment. If it would take a lot of time and effort to earn points on a particular question, make sure it is worthwhile to undertake this. If it is not, then click on Not Tracked/Unknown and move on. Your total score on the assessment may not be as high, but you will keep your momentum. It is not worth bending over backward to answer every question and identify every piece of data.

- [ ] **Delegate responsibility.** For example, your human resources manager might take the lead on figuring out how to implement a job-sharing program, and your COO might start gathering data on the environmental practices of your suppliers.

- [ ] **Talk to B Lab.** B Lab's staff members are available to review your assessment, answer your questions, and give you advice on how to improve your score, even if you are not seeking B Corp certification. I strongly encourage you to take advantage of this opportunity.

- [ ] **Submit your assessment (B Corps only).** An assessment review is a key part of the B Corp certification process. On this call, B Lab's staff will review each of your responses with you. The goal is to give you a better understanding of the intent behind each question and an idea of what it would take to implement that practice. Most businesses find that they make adjustments to their answers after they receive clarification from a B Lab staff member. Any representative of your company (e.g., an executive, an associate, or an intern) can complete this assessment review call.

Jed Davis, Director of Sustainability, Cabot Creamery
DAIRY PRODUCTS—VERMONT

Q: What business benefits do you directly attribute to your B Corp certification?

A: B Corp certification provides a unique perspective in answering the question "Are you operating your company in a sustainable way?" B Corp's focus on the organizational level, not merely at the level of our products, differentiates it among certifiers. Achieving B Corp certification also provides validation of a company's efforts to manage for sustainability, and the quality of the B Impact Assessment enhances the legitimacy and value of this third-party review. The process of completing the B Corp Assessment provides insights and guidance on areas of focus for continuous improvement.

Q: What was the biggest challenge you had to overcome to certify as a B Corp?

A: Initially B Corp's assessment was really better aligned for public or private companies who have shareholders as a major class of stakeholders. But as a testament to B Lab's work to constantly improve the B Corp Assessment, the tool now accommodates other business forms (in our case, a cooperative) and other business sizes equally well.

Q: What was your biggest surprise about becoming a B Corp?

A: Easy question to answer: the powerful fellowship among Certified B Corps. There is something special about companies that are B Corporations. Perhaps the element of the B the Change movement adds to this, but the B Corps as a lot are just so authentic, so eager, and so focused on aspirations to be "better." This reality has greatly surpassed our initial expectations in a wonderful way.

Week 4
Implement

Time Estimate: One to five hours.

OBJECTIVE: The objective during week 4 is for you and your team to dig in and start completing the items on your action plan.

END RESULT: An increase in your B Impact Assessment score.

☐ **Gather data and research.** Depending on your action plan, this is where you start identifying the financial, worker, supplier, community, and environmental data required to update your B Impact Assessment responses. If necessary, contact the people responsible for the data you need.[3]

☐ **Create policies and procedures.** One of the best ways to earn points on the B Impact Assessment is to formalize your policies and procedures in writing. For example, your company can earn points by creating an environmental purchasing policy, a local purchasing policy, a community service policy, an employee handbook, a whistle-blowing policy, a code of ethics, a supplier code of conduct, or an external annual report that details your mission-related performance.

RYAN'S TIP If you are seeking B Corp certification, a good practice is to ask yourself, "If I were audited, what written documentation do I have that could prove that my answer is correct?" In almost every case you'll need physical proof, not just informal practices, to qualify for points during the assessment review process.

Week 5
Fine-Tune

Time estimate: One to five hours.

OBJECTIVE: As your team is working through the action plan, keep track of your improvements by inserting your data into the B Impact Assessment. This will give you an updated score.

END RESULT: A recalculated and refined B Impact Assessment score.

- ☐ **Ready to tackle bigger items?** Depending on the measures you have implemented, the difficulty of those measures, and the results of the phone review with a B Lab staff member, your score may have improved since your initial assessment results. Now is a good time to reconnect with the key internal stakeholders in your company, such as the people you invited to the summit during week 2. Update these key stakeholders on your progress so far and have a conversation about the remaining (and possibly bigger) action items on your list. If you have not done so already, have a discussion about whether your company is interested in becoming a Certified B Corporation.

- ☐ **Next steps for B Corp certification (B Corps only).** After the phone review, did your score remain above 80 points? If your score dropped below 80, go back to the Improve Your Impact section in the B Impact Assessment to identify practices that can raise your score. The B Lab staff can give you recommendations to help you identify any low-hanging fruit. If your score stayed above 80, however, you can start submitting supporting documentation to verify your responses.

- ☐ **Submit supporting documentation (B Corps only).** After a B Lab staff member moves your assessment to the next stage of the review process, the B Impact Assessment will randomly select eight to twelve heavily weighted questions and ask you to submit supporting documentation to verify your responses. For example, if you said you have an environmental purchasing policy, B Lab's staff may ask you to upload that policy to the B Impact Assessment for review. Usually, the most heavily weighted questions are selected for verification. If your company is not able to verify a particular answer, the answer is changed and the credit is removed.

☐ **Make it official (B Corps only).** If the B Lab staff does not have any further questions about your uploaded documents, you are nearly finished. B Lab will send you an electronic version of the B Corp terms and conditions and the B Corporation Declaration of Interdependence and will ask you to pay the applicable B Corp certification fee.

Remind your staff to save any notes they have on why and how they answered certain questions on the assessment. These notes will come in handy if your company decides to become a B Corporation and you are asked to produce evidence of your practices.

Week 6
Celebrate and Next Steps

OBJECTIVE: By week 6, you will have made significant progress toward improving your social and environmental performance. If you have met the requirements to become a Certified B Corporation, congratulations on joining one of the most exciting and dynamic movements in business!

END RESULT: Celebrate, and congratulate your team for taking this journey.

☐ **Publicize your accomplishments.** Use this opportunity to share your success widely. Write an article in your company newsletter about your journey, accomplishments, and long-term plan. Try convening a "lunch and learn" with your staff to share your progress and encourage other employees to get involved. You also can publicize your achievement on your website, to engage your external stakeholders.

☐ **Consider building a stronger foundation.** In more than twenty-five U.S. states, including Delaware, the community of Certified B Corporations has helped pass legislation in support of a new corporate form called the benefit corporation. The benefit corporation gives entrepreneurs the freedom to consider shareholders, workers, suppliers, community, and the environment when making decisions. This helps ensure that your social and environmental mission can better survive new management, new investors, or even new ownership. See the appendix for additional details on the difference between Certified B Corporations and benefit corporations.

☐ **Focus on continual improvement.** Like many things in life, this is not a quick fix but a process of continual improvement. For example, does your team disband after this project is over? Will someone continue to be the internal champion? What other big picture goals do you want to strive for? Clarify how you and your team will continue to work toward achieving your social and environmental goals. Establish performance targets, and perhaps incentives, for achieving those ideal outcomes.

☐ **Check out the B Resources portal (B Corps only).** A great next step for new B Corporations is to visit the B Corp Resources Portal.[4] The resources portal has information on product and service discounts, tips on how to raise capital from mission-aligned investors, and a wide variety of tools to help you further improve your B Impact Assessment score.

Want to get the most out of your B Corp certification? I strongly believe that the key to maximizing the value of your certification is to make your involvement with the B Corp community a "top three" business priority. For example, B Corps in any sector—service, wholesale, retail, or manufacturing—can generate an incredible amount of thought leadership, business development, employee engagement, marketing opportunity, and innovative partnership entirely through utilizing the power and resources inherent in the B Corp community. This commitment to your fellow B Corps can make the difference between getting a great deal of value from your B Corp certification and wondering why you aren't getting more.

Jenn Vervier, Director of Strategy and Sustainability, New Belgium Brewing Company

CRAFT BREWED BEER AND ALES—COLORADO

Q: What business benefits do you directly attribute to your B Corp certification?

A: The biggest benefit is the ability to preserve our mission and culture against unsolicited tender offers. We don't have to worry that our board of directors might feel compelled to accept an offer that isn't in our overall best interests.

B Corp certification also further signals to our stakeholders (coworkers, customers, suppliers, and community) that our values are truly at the core of our business.

Q: What was the biggest challenge you had to overcome to certify as a B Corp?

A: We had to spend a little time to make sure we understood what the potential impact of B Corp certification would be on our ability to change our capital structure and on our valuation.

Q: What was your biggest surprise about becoming a B Corp?

A: I am deeply impressed by what a significant movement B Corps are becoming and the network of amazing brands that have been certified. I also appreciate how B Corps really seem to have each other's backs.

5

Conclusion

One Goal, Many Paths

I n a very short amount of time, the B Corporation movement has brought together a global community of innovative, passionate, and forward-thinking business leaders who are committed to solving some of the world's greatest social and environmental challenges. The rapid growth of the B Corp community, the legislative success with strong bipartisan approval, and the support of the investment community all are evidence that the idea of harnessing the power of business to drive systemic change is widely appealing.

As the same time, the B Corporation is not, and was never intended to be, the answer to all of our problems. The Certified B Corporation is one of many tools that can move us closer to the ultimate vision of a shared and durable prosperity. Indeed, some people may find that they prefer to work within other business or legal frameworks to meet their social and environmental goals. Debating which framework or movement is "best," however, misses the point. It does not matter which certification or framework we use, as long as it helps us alleviate poverty, build stronger communities, create better places to work, and protect the environment. The Certified B Corporation, in my opinion, is a brilliant concept, but it is not the only framework to help us achieve our end goal. There are many paths up the mountain.

Jay Coen Gilbert, Bart Houlahan, and Andrew Kassoy, the cofounders of B Lab, happily concede that the idea of using business as a force for good is not anything new. The B Corp community stands on the shoulders of more than fifty years of hard work in the microfinance, community development, cooperative ownership, clean tech, and socially responsible investing movements. The Certified B Corporation is the next iteration in a process of continual evolution.

What Does Success for the B Corp Movement Look Like?

Success for the B Corp movement is not necessarily rapid growth in the number of Certified B Corporations. Even if there were 100,000 Certified B Corps, this figure would represent only a small percentage of the total number of businesses worldwide.

A more valuable measurement of success, and perhaps the true legacy of the B Corp movement, would be a dramatic increase in the number of businesses that measure what matters (i.e., social and environmental performance in addition to financial performance) by using credible whole-business benchmarking tools such as the B Impact Assessment. When businesses measure the effects of their operations on all of their stakeholders, compare themselves with their industry peers, and start to compete to be the best *for* the world rather than just the best *in* the world, we will be making progress toward a shared and durable prosperity for all.

Success for the B Corp movement includes an increase in the percentage of new businesses that incorporate stakeholder interests into their foundational documents. Success includes more businesses measuring the social and environmental performance of their supply chains, helping suppliers to increase their overall performance, and using this impact data to make future procurement decisions. Success includes an increase in the number of business school graduates who work for companies that measure what matters. A growth in any of these figures—regardless of the total number of Certified B Corporations—would mean that creating value for workers, communities, and the environment, in addition to shareholders, is an idea that resonates with current and future entrepreneurs.

B THE CHANGE YOU WISH TO SEE IN THE WORLD. Come join the global movement to redefine success in business.

For me and for many of the other B Corporations with whom I have spoken, part of the fun is being on a common journey and feeling a deeply shared connection with so many interesting and caring people. The B Corp movement reconnected me with something that I had forgotten: the incredible power of being part of a community that shares my core values and a clear sense of purpose. Being part of this community—being part of a global movement of leaders who are using business as a force for good—motivates me to go to work each day.

Now that you've finished this book, the first step toward measuring what matters (or toward becoming a Certified B Corporation) is to take the B Impact Assessment. If you haven't already, I recommend giving the assessment a try and telling your friends, family, and colleagues about this free tool that can benchmark their companies' social and environmental performance.

I'll leave you with one of my favorite quotes, from Paul Hawken, one of the pioneers of the modern sustainability movement. I think his quote captures what we are collectively trying to achieve: "When asked if I am pessimistic or optimistic about the future, my answer is always the same: If you look at the science about what is happening on earth and aren't pessimistic, you don't understand data. But if you meet the people who are working to restore this earth and the lives of the poor, and you aren't optimistic, you haven't got a pulse. What I see everywhere in the world are ordinary people willing to confront despair, power, and incalculable odds in order to restore some semblance of grace, justice, and beauty to this world."[1]

I hope that you have enjoyed this book and have found it useful. If so, please spread the word. If you have questions or comments, you can always contact me directly.[2]

Appendix

Certified B Corporations and Benefit Corporations

What is the difference between a Certified B Corporation and a benefit corporation?

Certified B Corporations and benefit corporations are often, and understandably, confused. They share much in common but have a few important differences, as shown in the table.

Comparison of Certified B Corporations and Benefit Corporations

Requirement	Certified B Corporations	Benefit Corporations
Accountability	Directors are required to consider effects of decisions on shareholders *and* stakeholders	Same as Certified B Corporations
Transparency	Company must publish a public report assessing its overall impact against a third-party standard	Same as Certified B Corporations[a]
Performance	Verified by B Lab	Self-reported
Ongoing verification	Must recertify every two years	No ongoing verification other than transparency requirements
Support	Access to a portfolio of services and support from B Lab	No formal support from B Lab
Availability	Available to any private business in the world	Available only in specific countries (or specific U.S. states) that have passed benefit corporation legislation
Fees	Annual B Corp certification fees range from $500 to $25,000. Fees are calculated based on a company's annual sales	In the United States, state filing fees are typically between $70 and $200. Sample documents and information on finding an attorney are available at benefitcorp.net

a. Neither public reporting nor use of a third-party standard is currently required for Delaware benefit corporations. Details are available at bcorporation.net or benefitcorp.net.

Why was the benefit corporation legal structure created?

One of the primary challenges that the B Corp movement was created to address is the difficulty that many entrepreneurs have in raising capital, growing, or selling their business without diluting the company's original social and environmental values.

Through the leadership of B Lab and the community of Certified B Corps, laws have been passed in many states (and are moving forward in many more) to create a new type of corporation—the benefit corporation—that best meets the needs of entrepreneurs and investors seeking to use business to solve social and environmental problems while supporting sound financial performance.

Will becoming a benefit corporation affect my tax status?

In the United States, becoming a benefit corporation will not affect your company's tax status. Your company can still elect to be taxed as a C corp or S corp. Benefit corporation status affects only corporate purpose, accountability, and transparency requirements. Everything else remains the same.

Aren't companies such as Aveda already socially and environmentally responsible without a benefit corporation legal structure?

Companies such as Aveda, Ben & Jerry's, Burt's Bees, and Tom's of Maine proved that one can run a profitable business and have a social mission. However, in times of crisis, such as the recent financial collapse, or under a leadership change, social and environmental values can get pushed aside if they are not embedded in the company's foundational documents. The benefit corporation legal structure provides entrepreneurs, owners, and investors with the assurance that the company's social and environmental values will remain equally important to making a profit—no matter what.

How do I become a benefit corporation in the United States?

If you are starting a new company, you can incorporate as a benefit corporation in any state where benefit corporation legislation has been passed. The procedure is nearly identical to that followed for any other corporate structure. If you have an existing company, you can elect to become a benefit corporation by amending your company's governing documents.

What types of companies can become Certified B Corporations?

Nonprofits, such as 501c(3)s in the United States, and government agencies are not eligible to become B Corps. Companies with any of the following corporate structures may become Certified B Corps:

- Benefit corporation
- C corporation
- Cooperative
- Employee stock ownership plan (ESOP)
- For-profit company outside the United States
- Limited liability company (LLC)
- Low-profit limited liability company (L3C)
- Partnership
- S corporation
- Sole proprietorship
- Wholly-owned subsidiary

A more thorough discussion of the need for and rationale behind the benefit corporation, state-by-state instructions, and detailed technical information about benefit corporations is available through the Benefit Corp Information Center website, benefitcorp.net.

Notes

Foreword

1. CalPERS Sustainable Investment Research Initiative, *Review of Evidence: Database of Academic Studies,* June 2013, http://www.calpers-governance.org/docs-sof/investments /siri-database-of-academic-studies.pdf.

Introduction

1. *Inc., How a Business Can Change the World,* http://www.inc.com/magazine/20110501 /how-a-business-can-change-the-world.html; Tina Rosenberg, "Ethical Businesses with a Better Bottom Line," *New York Times,* April 14, 2011, http://opinionator.blogs.nytimes .com/2011/04/14/ethical-businesses-with-a-better-bottom-line.

2. The B Impact Assessment is available online at bimpactassessment.net.

3. Visit honeymanconsulting.com/book to learn more.

Part 1: Overview

1. Goldman Sachs, *GS Sustain,* June 22, 2007: 12, http://www.natcapsolutions.org /business-case/GoldmanSachsReport_v2007.pdf.

2. International Finance Corporation, *The Business Case for Sustainability,* 2012: 4, http://www.ifc.org/wps/wcm/connect/9519a5004c1bc60eb534bd79803d5464 /Business%2BCase%2Bfor%2BSustainability.pdf?MOD=AJPERES.

3. Robert G. Eccles, Ioannis Ioannou, and George Serafeim, *The Impact of Corporate Sustainability on Organizational Processes and Performance,* November 23, 2013: 1, http://ssrn.com/abstract=1964011.

4. Peter Lacy, Tim Cooper, Rob Hayward, and Lisa Neuberger, *A New Era of Sustainability: UN Global Compact-Accenture CEO Study 2010,* 2010 (June): 10, http://www.accenture.com /SiteCollectionDocuments/PDF/Accenture_A_New_Era_of_Sustainability_CEO_Study.pdf.

5. Deloitte, *Sustainability: Balancing Opportunity and Risk in the Consumer Product Industry,* 2007: 1, http://www.natcapsolutions.org/business-case/Deloitte2007business-case.pdf.

6. PricewaterhouseCoopers and SAM, *The Sustainability Yearbook 2008,* 2008: 24, http:// www.natcapsolutions.org/business-case/Sustainability_Yearbook_BusinessCase2008.pdf.

7. Sheila Bonini and Stephan Görner, "Putting It into Practice," *The Business of Sustainability: McKinsey Global Survey Results,* 2011: 6, http://www.mckinsey.com/insights /energy_resources_materials/the_business_of_sustainability_mckinsey_global_survey _results.

8. Goldman Sachs, *GS Sustain,* 21. For an impressive compilation of credible studies on the business case for sustainability, including studies from A. T. Kearney, Deloitte, the Economist Intelligence Unit, Gallup, *Harvard Business Review,* the Massachusetts Institute of Technology, McKinsey, the U.S. Department of Energy, and many others, I highly

recommend reading Natural Capitalism Solutions, *Sustainability Pays: Studies that Prove the Business Case for Sustainability,* http://www.natcapsolutions.org/businesscasereports.pdf. Also available at honeymanconsulting.com/book.

9. Rick Warren, *The Purpose-Driven Life* (Grand Rapids, MI: Zondervan, 2002).

10. Jay Coen Gilbert, "Can I Get a Witness?! The Evolution of Capitalism," *Huffington Post,* September 27, 2011, http://www.huffingtonpost.com/jay-coen-gilbert/benefit -corporation-legislation-_b_976650.html.

Part 2: Ten Benefits of Becoming a B Corp

1. Goldman Sachs, *GS Sustain,* 21.

2. "Millennials in the Workforce: A Work–Life Integration," *YPULSE,* February 20, 2013, http://www.ypulse.com/post/view/millennials-in-the-workforce-work-life-integration.

3. Lindsay Gellman and Rachel Feintzeig, "Social Seal of Approval Lures Talent," *The Wall Street Journal,* November 12, 2013, http://online.wsj.com/news/articles /SB10001424052702304868404579193973525834320.

4. For more details on how Etsy used the B Impact Assessment to increase employee initiative, motivation, and innovation while pushing its company to the next level of social and environmental performance, see Jay Coen Gilbert, "Etsy's Hackathon for Good," *Harvard Business Review,* November 14, 2012, http://blogs.hbr.org/2012/11/etsys-hackathon -for-good/.

5. Simon Sinek, "How Great Leaders Inspire Action," TED video, 18:04, from TEDxPuget Sound, September 2009, https://www.ted.com/talks/simon_sinek_how_great_leaders _inspire_action.

6. Seth Godin, "Toward Zero Unemployment," *Seth's Blog,* March 27, 2013, http://sethgodin .typepad.com/seths_blog/2013/03/toward-zero-unemployment-.html.

7. www.bcorporation.net.

8. Goldman Sachs, *GS Sustain,* 22.

9. Michelle Goodman, "Everything You Need to Know about B Corporation Certification," *Entrepreneur,* August 6, 2013, http://www.entrepreneur.com/article/227099.

10. At the 2013 B Corp Champions Retreat, Etsy received a Race to the Top award for improving its B Impact Score from just over 80 to 105 during its first year of certification.

11. See www.sistemab.org.

12. See marsdd.com.

Part 3: The B Impact Assessment

1. For the full version of the B Impact Assessment, visit bimpactassessment.net. To get a quick snapshot of your impact, visit bimpactassessment.net/quick.

2. Visit www.bcorporation.net to view the most recent fee structure.

3. To view an example, see King Arthur Flour's 2012 B Impact Report at honeymanconsulting .com/book or bimpactassessment.net.

4. If you need direct assistance, feel free to call B Lab at (610) 293-0299 or e-mail thelab @bcorporation.net.

5. Goldman Sachs, *GS Sustain,* 7, 47.

6. For anecdotal compensation rates for companies in your industry, visit www.glassdoor.com.

7. "Fortune 50 CEO Pay vs. Our Salaries," *CNN Money,* http://money.cnn.com/magazines/ fortune/fortune500/2012/ceo-pay-ratios/.

8. John Mackey and Raj Sisodia, *Conscious Capitalism: Liberating the Heroic Spirit of Business* (Boston: Harvard Business Review Press, 2013), 95.

9. Stephen Miller, "Socially Responsible Funds Popular in Mission-Driven 401(k)s," *Society for Human Resource Management,* September 30, 2001, http://www.shrm.org /hrdisciplines/benefits/Articles/Pages/SRIfunds.aspx.

10. Daniel H. Pink, *Drive: The Surprising Truth about What Motivates Us* (New York: Riverhead Books, 2009).

11. Tony Hsieh, *Delivering Happiness: A Path to Profits, Passion, and Purpose* (New York: Business Plus, 2010), 233.

12. Leonard L. Berry, Ann M. Mirabito, and William B. Baun, "What's the Hard Return on Employee Wellness Program?," *Harvard Business Review,* December 1, 2010, http://hbr.org/2010/12/whats-the-hard-return-on-employee-wellness-programs/ar/1.

13. Yvon Chouinard, *Let My People Go Surfing: The Education of a Reluctant Businessman* (New York: Penguin, 2006), 174.

14. Mackey and Sisodia, *Conscious Capitalism,* 95.

15. Nikki Blacksmith and Jim Harter, "Majority of American Workers Not Engaged in Their Jobs," *Gallup,* October 28, 2011, http://www.gallup.com/poll/150383/Majority-American -Workers-Not-Engaged-Jobs.aspx.

16. Jim Harter and Sangeeta Agrawal, "Actively Disengaged Workers and Jobless in Equally Poor Health," *Gallup,* April 20, 2011, http://www.gallup.com/poll/147191/Actively -Disengaged-Workers-Jobless-Equally-Poor-Health.aspx.

17. Blacksmith and Harter, "Majority of American Workers Not Engaged."

18. Coro Strandberg, *Credit Union Social Responsibility: A Sustainability Road Map,* Filene Research Institute, 2010: 54, http://filene.org/assets/pdf-reports/207_Strandberg _Sustainability_Road_Map.pdf.

19. Steven Greenhouse, "Flex Time Flourishes in Accounting Industry," *New York Times,* January 7, 2011, http://www.nytimes.com/2011/01/08/business/08perks .html?pagewanted=all&_r=0.

20. McKinsey & Company, *Gender Diversity in Top Management: Moving Corporate Culture, Moving Boundaries,* 2013, http://www.mckinsey.com/~/media/McKinsey/dotcom /homepage/2012_March_Women_Matter/PDF/WomenMatter%202013%20Report.ashx.

21. Credit Suisse, *Gender Diversity and Corporate Performance*, August 2012, https://www .credit-suisse.com/newsletter/doc/gender_diversity.pdf.

22. Kirk Snyder, "Bringing the Outsiders In," *The Guardian*, September 8, 2006, http://www .theguardian.com/money/2006/sep/09/gayfinance.careers.

23. 2020 Women on Boards, *2020 Gender Diversity Index: 2013 Key Findings*, http://www.2020wob.com/sites/default/files/2020GDI-2013Report.pdf.

24. *Idealist*, "Why Is Volunteering Important?,"http://www.idealist.org/info/Volunteer/Why.

25. Steven A. Rochlin and Brenda Christoffer, *Making the Business Case: Determining the Value of Corporate Community Involvement* (Boston: The Center for Corporate Citizenship at Boston College, 2000), http://commdev.org/files/750_file_making_the_business_case.pdf.

26. Michael Tuffrey, *Good Companies, Better Employees: How Community Involvement and Good Corporate Citizenship Can Enhance Employee Morale, Motivation, Commitment, and Performance* (London: The Corporate Citizenship Company, 2003), http://www.centrica .com/files/reports/2005cr/files/csr_good_companies_better_employees.pdf.

27. Contact thelab@bcorporation.net for more information.

28. Cohn and Wolfe, *From Transparency to Full Disclosure*, October 2013, 8, http://www .cohnwolfe.com/sites/default/files/reprinted%20articles/Cohn%20&%20Wolfe%20 -%20From%20Transparency%20to%20Full%20Disclosure%20report.pdf.

29. Paul Griffin and Yuan Sun, *Going Green: Market Reaction to CSR Newswire Releases*, January 29, 2012, doi: 10.2139/SSRN 1995132.

30. Carbon Disclosure Project, *CDP Global 500 Report 2011: Accelerating Low Carbon Growth*, https://www.cdp.net/en-US/Results/Pages/CDP-Global-500-Report-2011.aspx?PageID=1.

31. bimpactassessment.net.

32. Bonini and Görner, *Putting It into Practice*, 6.

33. www.energystar.gov.

34. Visit www.earth911.org to find a location near you that accepts universal wastes.

35. Brian Carr, "Commute Options Programs Increase Employee Satisfaction, Retention," *HR.com*, November 3, 2011. http://www.hr.com/en/app/blog/2011/11/commute-options -programs-increase-employee-satisfa_gujwyz6m.html.

36. www.energystar.gov.

37. www.ghgprotocol.org.

38. www.bcorporation.net/how or benefitcorp.net also can provide detailed information that is relevant to your specific situation.

39. William McDonough and Michael Braungart, *Cradle to Cradle: Remaking the Way We Make Things* (New York: North Point Press, 2002), 9.

40. bimpactassessment.net.

41. Adapted from C. K. Prahalad, *Fortune at the Bottom of the Pyramid: Eradicating Poverty through Profits* (New York: DK Publishing, 2006).

42. Adapted from "Fair Trade Standards," *Fair Trade USA*, http://fairtradeusa.org/certification /standards.

Part 4: The Quick Start Guide

1. See www.bcorporation.net for more details.

2. Visit honeymanconsulting.com/book or bimpactassessment.net to download a sample action plan created by Dancing Deer Baking Company.

3. Visit honeymanconsulting.com/book or bimpactassessment.net to download an improvement report created by Greyston Bakery.

4. www.bcorporation.net.

Part 5: Conclusion

1. Paul Hawken, "Commencement: Healing or Stealing," 2009 commencement address, University of Portland, http://www.up.edu/commencement/default.aspx?cid=9456.

2. ryan@honeymanconsulting.com.

Resources

The B Corp Resource List

Online Resources

The B Corp Resource List is a collection of articles, templates, best practice ideas, books, business school case studies, TED Talks, and videos to help you build a better business and learn more about the B Corp movement. All of the articles, templates, videos, and other resources listed in the following section are hosted online at **honeymanconsulting.com/book**. This online list will be continually updated as new B Corp resources become available.

Good for Workers

Compensation, Benefits, and Wages

Green America: *How to Add a Socially and Environmentally Responsible Investment Option to an Employer's Retirement Plan*

Nolo Press: *Outplacement Programs for Laid-Off Workers*

———: *Should You Offer Severance Pay?*

Worker Ownership

The Guardian: How to Implement Employee Ownership

Inc.: Employee Ownership 101

National Center for Employee Ownership: *An Introduction to the World of Employee Ownership*

Work Environment

B Resource Guide: *Creating a Code of Ethics*

———: *Creating an Employee Handbook*

———: *Creating an Employee Wellness Program*

———: *Employee Engagement and Metrics*

———: *Employee Wellness: iContact*

———: *Worker Health and Safety*

Entrepreneur: *The Basics of Employee Benefits*

Families and Work Institute: *Workplace Flexibility: A Guide for Companies*

FindLaw: *Sample Anti-Discrimination and Harassment Policy*

Harvard Business Review: *Etsy's Hackathon for Good*

Inc.: *Sample Employee Satisfaction Survey*

———: *Nine Avoidable Workplace Health and Safety Hazards*

———: *Sample Employee Review Questionnaire*

———: *Tools for Creating an Employee Handbook*

U.S. Department of Labor: *Workplace Flexibility Toolkit*

U.S. Small Business Administration: *Optional Employee Benefits*

Good for the Community

Job Creation
B Resource Guide: *Worker Training and Education*

Diversity
Center for Talent Innovation: *Innovation, Diversity, and Market Growth*

Forbes: *Fostering Innovation through a Diverse Workforce*

Civic Engagement and Giving
B Resource Guide: *Community Service Programs*

Charities Aid Foundation: *Engaging Employees with Charity Partnerships*

Inc.: *How to Start a Volunteer Program*

U.S. Better Business Bureau: *Reviews of Charities and Donors*

Local Involvement
B Resource Guide: *How to Write and Implement a Local Purchasing Policy*

Green America: *Ten Steps to Break Up with Your Mega-Bank*

Suppliers, Distributors, and Product
B Resource Guide: *Conducting a Supplier Survey*

Good for the Environment

Land, Office, and Plant

B Resource Guide: *Best Practices to Manage Product Toxicity*

——: *Conducting Environmental Audits*

——: *Monitoring and Recording Hazardous and Nonhazardous Waste*

CarbonFund: *Responsible Purchasing Guide for Carbon Offsets*

Energy Star: *Energy Strategies for Buildings and Plants*

U.S. Environmental Protection Agency: *A Guide to Indoor Air Quality*

——: *Guide to Purchasing Green Power*

——: *Quick Tips to Make Your Small Business Efficient*

——: *Renewable Energy Certificates*

——: *WaterSense Program for Commercial Facilities*

Energy, Water, and Materials

B Resource Guide: *Conducting a Life Cycle Assessment*

U.S. Environmental Protection Agency: *LCA Resources*

Emissions and Waste

B Resource Guide: *Calculating Greenhouse Gas Emissions*

——: *Reducing Material Usage*

EPA SmartWay: *Efficient Shipping*

Greenhouse Gas Protocol: *Calculation Tools*

Renewable Choice Energy: *Business Carbon Footprint Calculator*

Transport, Distribution, and Suppliers

Carbon Disclosure Project: *CDP Supply Chain Program*

U.S. Environmental Protection Agency: *Managing Supply Chain GHG Emissions*

Good for the Long Term

Mission and Engagement

B Resource Guide: *Creating and Improving Your Audit Committee*

——: *Implementing Financial Controls*

Inc.: How to Build a Board of Directors

——: *How to Institute an Employee Review Process*

——: *Sample Employee Performance Review Form*

Transparency

Ben & Jerry's: *Social and Environmental Report*

Give Something Back Office Supplies: *Annual Giving Report*

Greyston Bakery: *Annual Benefit Report*

The Redwoods Group: *Social Audit*

Good to the Core

Shareable: *How to Start a Worker Co-op*

Books by (or about) B Corps

Ben & Jerry's

Cohen, Ben, and Jerry Greenfield. *Double Dip: How to Run a Values-Led Business and Make Money, Too*. New York: Simon & Shuster, 1998.

Edmondson, Brad. *Ice Cream Social: The Struggle for the Soul of Ben & Jerry's*. San Francisco: Berrett-Koehler Publishers, 2014.

Lager, Fred. *The Inside Scoop: How Two Real Guys Built a Business with a Social Conscience and a Sense of Humor*. New York: Three Rivers Press, 1995.

Biomimicry Group

Benyus, Janine. *Biomimicry: Innovation Inspired by Nature*. New York: William Morrow, 1997.

CSRwire

Mager, David, and Joe Sibila. *Street Smart Sustainability: The Entrepreneur's Guide to Profitably Greening Your Organization's DNA*. San Francisco: Berrett-Koehler Publishers, 2010.

Cutting Edge Capital

Shuman, Michael. *Local Dollars, Local Sense: How to Shift Your Money from Wall Street to Main Street and Achieve Real Prosperity*. White River Junction, VT: Chelsea Green, 2012.

Shuman, Michael. *The Small Mart Revolution: How Local Businesses Are Beating the Global Competition.* San Francisco: Berrett-Koehler Publishers, 2007.

Greyston Bakery

Lynch, Kevin, and Julius Walls. *Mission, Inc.: The Practitioners Guide to Social Enterprise.* San Francisco: Berrett-Koehler Publishers, 2008.

Jitasa

Russell, Jeff. *Do What You Do Best: Outsourcing as Capacity Building in the Nonprofit Sector.* Boise, ID: Elevate, 2013.

Mal Warwick Associates

Cohen, Ben, and Mal Warwick. *Values-Driven Business: How to Change the World, Make Money, and Have Fun.* San Francisco: Berrett-Koehler Publishers, 2006.

Polak, Paul, and Mal Warwick. *The Business Solution to Poverty: Designing Products and Services for Three Billion New Customers.* San Francisco: Berrett-Koehler Publishers, 2013.

Method

Lowry, Adam, and Eric Ryan. *The Method Method: Seven Obsessions that Helped Our Scrappy Start-Up Turn an Industry Upside Down.* New York: Penguin Portfolio, 2011.

———. *Squeaky Green: The Method Guide to Detoxing Your Home.* San Francisco: Chronicle Books, 2008.

Metropolitan Group

Conley, Chip, and Eric Friedenwald-Fishman. *Marketing that Matters: 10 Practices to Profit Your Business and Change the World.* San Francisco: Berrett-Koehler Publishers, 2006.

Montgomery & Hansen

Montgomery, John. *Great from the Start: How Conscious Corporations Attract Success.* New York: Morgan James, 2012.

Mosaic

Aujila, Dev, and Billy Parish. *Making Good: Finding Meaning, Money, and Community in a Changing World.* Emmaus, PA: Rodale, 2012.

Ogden Publications

Welch, Bryan. *Beautiful and Abundant: Building the World We Want.* Lawrence, KS: B&A Books, 2010.

Patagonia

Chouinard, Yvon. *Let My People Go Surfing: The Education of a Reluctant Businessman*. London: Penguin Books, 2006.

Chouinard, Yvon, and Vincent Stanley. *The Responsible Company: What We've Learned from Patagonia's First 40 Years*. Ventura, CA: Patagonia Books, 2012.

Seventh Generation

Breen, Bill, Jeffrey Hollender, and Peter Senge. *The Responsibility Revolution: How the Next Generation of Businesses Will Win*. San Francisco: Jossey-Bass, 2010.

Catling, Linda, and Jeffrey Hollender. *How to Make the World a Better Place: 116 Ways You Can Make a Difference*. New York: W. W. Norton & Company, 2013.

Davis, Geoff, Jeffrey Hollender, and Meika Hollender. *Naturally Clean: The Seventh Generation Guide to Safe & Healthy, Non-Toxic Cleaning*. Gabriola Island, British Columbia: New Society Publishers, 2006.

Hollender, Jeffrey. *In Our Every Deliberation: An Introduction to Seventh Generation*. Burlington, VT: Seventh Generation, 2009.

———. *What Matters Most: How a Small Group of Pioneers Is Teaching Social Responsibility to Big Business, and Why Big Business Is Listening*. New York: Basic Books, 2006.

Hollender, Jeffrey, and John Hollender. *How to Make the World a Better Place: A Guide to Doing Good*. New York: Quill, 1990.

Hollender, Jeffrey, and Wayne Visser. *The Age of Responsibility: CSR 2.0 and the New DNA of Business*. New York: Wiley, 2011.

Hollender, Jeffrey, and Alexandra Zissu. *Planet Home: Conscious Choices for Cleaning and Greening the World You Care About Most*. New York: Clarkson Potter, 2010.

South Mountain Company

Abrams, John, and William Grieder. *The Company We Keep: Reinventing Business for People, Community, and Place*. White River Junction, VT: Chelsea Green, 2005.

Sungevity

Kennedy, Danny. *Rooftop Revolution: How Solar Power Can Save Our Economy—and Our Planet—from Dirty Energy*. San Francisco: Berrett-Koehler Publishers, 2012.

Sustainability Advantage

Elkington, John, and Bob Willard. *The Sustainability Advantage: Seven Business Case Benefits of a Triple Bottom Line.* Gabriola Island, British Columbia: New Society Publishers, 2002.

Willard, Bob. *The Next Sustainability Wave: Building Boardroom Buy-In.* Gabriola Island, British Columbia: New Society Publishers, 2005.

———. *The Sustainability Champion's Guidebook: How to Transform Your Company.* Gabriola Island, British Columbia: New Society Publishers, 2009.

The Honest Company

Alba, Jessica. *The Honest Life: Living Naturally and True to You.* Emmaus, PA: Rodale, 2013.

Gavigan, Christopher. *Healthy Child Healthy World: Creating a Cleaner, Greener, Safer Home.* New York: Plume, 2009.

Volans

Elkington, John. *Cannibals with Forks: The Triple Bottom Line of 21st Century Business.* Gabriola Island, British Columbia: New Society Publishers, 1998.

———. *The Zeronauts: Breaking the Sustainability Barrier.* New York: Routledge, 2012.

Elkington, John, Marc J. Epstein, and Herman B. Leonard. *Making Sustainability Work: Best Practices in Managing and Measuring Corporate Social, Environmental, and Economic Impacts.* San Francisco: Berrett-Koehler Publishers, 2008.

Elkington, John, Pamela Hartigan, and Klaus Schwab. *The Power of Unreasonable People: How Social Entrepreneurs Create Markets that Change the World.* Boston: Harvard Business Review Press, 2008.

Elkington, John, and Jochen Zeitz. *The Breakthrough Challenge: 10 Ways to Connect Today's Profits with Tomorrow's Bottom Line.* New York: Jossey-Bass, 2014.

Business School Case Studies by (or about) B Corps

Links to the following case studies are at **honeymanconsulting.com/book**.

Agora Partnerships

Cortes, Rocio Sanz, and Olav Sorenson. *Agora Partnerships: Investing with Impact.* Yale School of Management, 2013.

Lazzaroni, Mario. *Agora Partnerships: Structuring a Seed Stage Investment in Nicaragua*. INCAE Business School, 2005.

Ben & Jerry's

Austin, James, and James Quinn. *Ben & Jerry's: Preserving Mission and Brand within Unilever*. Harvard Business School, 2005.

Bourgeois, L. J., Elio Mariani, and Vivian Jen Yu. *Ben & Jerry's and Unilever: The Bohemian and the Behemoth*. Darden School of Business, 2004.

Child, Curtis, and Eva Witesman. *Institutional Choice Redux: How Fair Trade Entrepreneurs Choose Between Nonprofit and For-Profit Forms*. Brigham Young University, 2012.

Collins, David J., and Melinda B. Conrad. *Ben & Jerry's Homemade Ice Cream, Inc.: A Period of Transition*. Harvard Business School, 1996.

Hagen, James M. *Ben & Jerry's—Japan*. Richard Ivey School of Business, 2000.

Mead, Jenny, Robert J. Sack, and Pat Werhane. *Ben & Jerry's Homemade, Inc. (A): Acquisition Suitors at the Door*. Darden School of Business, 2002.

——. *Ben & Jerry's Homemade, Inc. (B): Scooped Up! What Lies Ahead?* Darden School of Business, 2001. (Revised 2008.)

Schill, Michael J. *Ben & Jerry's Homemade*. Darden School of Business, 2002.

Theroux, John. *Ben & Jerry's Homemade Ice Cream, Inc.: Keeping the Mission(s) Alive*. Harvard Business School, 1991.

Better World Books

Avery, Jill, Michael L. Norton, Fiona Wilson, and Thomas Steenburgh. *Better World Books*. Harvard Business School, 2010. (Revised 2012.)

Hess, Edward D., and Gosia Glinska. *Better World Books*. Darden School of Business, 2010.

Jones, Jamie, Jennifer Yee, and Wes Selke. *Good Capital and Better World Books: A Better World for Investing*. Kellogg School of Management, 2010.

Community Wealth Ventures

Austin, James E., and Meredith D. Pearson. *Community Wealth Ventures, Inc.* Harvard Business School, 1998.

Guayaki, Larry's Beans, Patagonia, Salt Spring Coffee

Craig, Alexander, Katja Macura, and Giancarlo Pucci. *Purposeful Action: Organizational Practices that Contribute to a Culture of Strategic Decision Making for Sustainability.* Blekinge Institute of Technology, 2012.

Ignia

Chu, Michael, Carlos Danel, and Robert C. Loudermilk Jr. *Play It Safe at Home, or Take a Risk Abroad?* Harvard Business School, 2012.

Impact Makers

Hess, Edward D., Jenny Mead, and Pat Werhane. *Impact Makers.* Darden School of Business, 2009.

King Arthur Flour

DeLong, Thomas, James Holian, and Joshua Weiss. *King Arthur Flour.* Harvard Business School, 2006. (Revised 2007.)

Movirtu

London, Ted. *Movirtu's Cloud Phone Service: Funding a Base-of-the-Pyramid Venture.* ERB Institute at the University of Michigan, 2012.

Patagonia

Johnson, Allyson, Courtney Lee, Steven Rippberger, and Morgane Treanton. *Patagonia: Encouraging Customers to Buy Used Clothing.* ERB Institute at the University of Michigan, 2012.

Pura Vida Coffee

Austin, James E., and Allen Grossman. *Pura Vida Coffee.* Harvard Business School, 2002.

Roshan

Leonard, Herman B., and Qahir Dhanani. *Roshan: Light at the End of the Tunnel in Afghanistan.* Harvard Business School, 2009. (Revised 2010.)

Seventh Generation

Raufflet, Emmanuel, and Mihaela Stefanov. *Seventh Generation: The Marketside Offer.* Harvard Business School, 2010.

VeeV

Margolis, Joshua D., Christopher Marquis, and Laura Winig. *VeeV on the Rocks?* Harvard Business School, 2009. (Revised 2011.)

TED Talks or Videos by B Corps

Links to the following videos are available at **honeymanconsulting.com/book**.

B Lab
Gilbert, Jay Coen. "On Better Business." TEDxPhiladelphia, 2010.

Cascade Engineering
Keller, Fred. "Why Business? Why Now?" TEDxGrandRapids, 2013.

CSRHub
Figge, Cynthia. "Applied Peace Innovation." TEDxHayward, 2013.

institute B
institute B. *Not Business as Usual.* 2014.

Montgomery & Hansen
Montgomery, John. "Benefit Corporation." TEDxHultBusinessSchoolSF, 2012.

———. "How Conscious Corporations Attract Success." TEDxLowerEastSide, 2014.

New Belgium Brewing Company
Jordan, Kim. "Brewing Happy Employees." TEDxFortCollins, 2011.

Patagonia
Sheahan, Casey. "The Next Industrial Revolution." TEDxMileHigh, 2011.

Rally Software
Martens, Ryan. "Solving for Why." TEDxMileHigh, 2012.

Roshan
Khoja, Shainoor. "Are You Making a Difference?" TEDxBGI, 2013.

TMI Consulting
Jana, Tiffany. "The Power of Privilege." TEDxRVAWomen, 2014.

Acknowledgments

I am forever grateful to the dozens of inspiring, loving, and supportive people who helped me write this book. In particular, I want to say thank you,

- to the entire B Corp community; it is—and always was—about you.
- to the hundreds of B Corps who contributed their voices; your stories make this book come to life.
- to the entire B Lab team, especially Jay Coen Gilbert, Hardik Savalia, and Katie Kerr, who worked selflessly and tirelessly to help me complete this book.
- to all the B Corps who read (and reread) my manuscript, including Mandy Cabot, Tim Frick, Anders Ferguson, Rebecca Hamilton, Kim Coupounas, Jed Davis, Rob Michalak, John Replogle, Bryan Welch, Chris Mann, Bec McHenry, Elisa Miller-Out, Nancy Goldstein, Nadia Woodhouse, Terri Rosenstock, Merlin Clarke, Annabel Adams, Drew Tulchin, Bruce Taylor, Ashley King, Nancy Vollmer, Beth Carls, Matt Mayer, Rob Sinclair, Ahmed Rahim, Dermot Hikisch, Ben Anderson, Victoria Fiore, Pam Hausner, Amy Haddon, Danielle Cresswell, Sunil Unikkat, Lyle Estill, and many others.
- to my top-notch editor, Neal Maillet, and the entire team at Berrett-Koehler, who went above and beyond what any other publisher would have done for this book, and whose wisdom, feedback, and flexibility were invaluable.
- to Jerrod Modica, the art director for *The B Corp Handbook,* and the T2AP/ Ammirati team, who made this publication incredibly creative and engaging.
- and finally, to my wife, whose unwavering love, support, and health insurance made this book possible.

I could not have done it without any of you. Thank you!

Index

Photo Credits

About the Nonprofit Behind B Corps

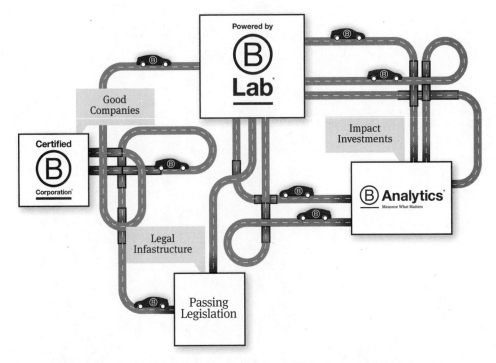

B Lab is a nonprofit organization that serves a global movement to redefine success in business so that one day all companies will compete not only to be the best *in* the world, but the best *for* the world.

B Lab drives this systemic change by:

1) building a community of Certified B Corporations to make it easier for all of us to tell the difference between "good companies" and good marketing;

2) passing benefit corporation legislation to give business leaders the freedom to create value for society as well as shareholders;

3) helping businesses measure, compare, and improve their social and environmental performance using the free B Impact Assessment; and

4) driving capital to impact investments through use of its B Analytics and Global Impact Investing Ratings System (GIIRS) Ratings platform.

B Lab was awarded the Skoll Award in Social Entrepreneurship in 2014.

Interested in collaboration? You can contact the folks at B Lab at 610-293-0299 or email at thelab@bcorporation.net.

About the Author

Ryan Honeyman is a consultant, executive coach, keynote speaker, author, and founder of Honeyman Sustainability Consulting, a Certified B Corporation. Ryan helps businesses save money, improve employee satisfaction, and increase brand value by helping them maximize the value of their sustainability efforts, including helping companies certify and thrive as B Corps. His clients include Ben & Jerry's, Klean Kanteen, Nutiva, McEvoy Ranch, Opticos Design, CleanWell, Exygy, and the Filene Research Institute.

Honeyman Sustainability Consulting has been honored—alongside GoLite, Method, New Belgium Brewing Company, Patagonia, and Seventh Generation—on the B Corp Best for the Environment list, which recognizes businesses that have scored in the top 10 percent of all B Corps worldwide for positive environmental impact. Ryan has also been honored twice by B Lab, the nonprofit organization that certifies B Corporations and stewards the movement, as a recipient of a B Corp Champion award for his leadership in fostering collaboration among the B Corp community.

Ryan has written articles for *Utne Reader, Sustainable Industries,* and *Triple-Pundit.* He also has been a featured speaker at the California College of the Arts, Chabot College, Golden Gate University, Mills College, San Francisco State University, The Haas School of Business at the University of California Berkeley, and The Wharton School of the University of Pennsylvania.

Ryan holds a bachelor's degree from the University of California, Santa Cruz, and a master's degree from the London School of Economics and Political Science.

You can contact Ryan directly at ryan@honeymanconsulting.com.

Berrett–Koehler
Publishers

Berrett–Koehler
Publishers

A community dedicated to creating
a world that works for all

Dear Reader,

Thank you for picking up this book and joining our worldwide community of Berrett-Koehler readers. We share ideas that bring positive change into people's lives, organizations, and society.

To welcome you, we'd like to offer you a free e-book. You can pick from among twelve of our bestselling books by entering the promotional code **BKP92E** here: http://www.bkconnection.com/welcome.

When you claim your free e-book, we'll also send you a copy of our e-newsletter, the *BK Communiqué*. Although you're free to unsubscribe, there are many benefits to sticking around. In every issue of our newsletter you'll find

- A free e-book
- Tips from famous authors
- Discounts on spotlight titles
- Hilarious insider publishing news
- A chance to win a prize for answering a riddle

Best of all, our readers tell us, "Your newsletter is the only one I actually read." So claim your gift today, and please stay in touch!

Sincerely,

Charlotte Ashlock
Steward of the BK Website

Questions? Comments? Contact me at bkcommunity@bkpub.com.